EMPOWERED

To Make A

DIFFERENCE

By
LES TRIPP

ISBN: 978-1-963565-82-9 (Paperback)
ISBN: 978-1-963565-86-7 (eBook)

Library of Congress Control Number: 2025904954

Printed in the United States of America

Published by:

info@thequippyquill.com
(302) 295-2278

Empowered to Make a Difference stresses how God enables believers to advance his kingdom in their own lives and in the lives of others. Les Tripp identifies the role of the Spirit to bring people into his family, lead them to surrender their lives, gift them uniquely to do his will, and work through them to achieve his purpose for their lives. A must-read for those desiring a closer walk with the Lord.

Fred G. King, Retired Pastor,
Ensley Church, Pensacola, FL

God wants to be intimately involved in the lives of believers. His intent is to work through us to build God's kingdom. For us, the tasks are impossible. The good news, as Les points out, is that God does not expect us to build his kingdom on our own but accomplishes this through his indwelling Spirit. This book brings insight and clarity to the working of the Spirit within believers. May God enrich your life and lead you to a deeper experience in Him.

Robert Young, Pastor, Mentor, Discipler,
International Speaker, and Friend

Les Tripp directs the reader to the importance of being filled with the Holy Spirit so that one can live healthy, productive lives. *Empowered to Make a Difference* is about the Spirit's involvement in one's life to bring peace, contentment, and purpose while equipping readers to accomplish God's will. Readers will be rewarded by time reflecting on and applying the truths presented here.

Chuck Brewster, Founder and President,
Champions of Honor and author of *Dead Men Rising*

In *Empowered to Make a Difference*, Les Tripp clearly lays out the path from salvation to disciple-making. He makes clear the difference between "being in Christ" and experiencing "Christ in me." This is a must-read for believers who want to break free of excuses and objections that keep them from being productive members of their kingdom. This book will help the believer understand the power of God available to believers.

Marty Granger, Founder and President

Ministry Alliance

This book is dedicated to my grandchildren:

Jimmy
Nicole
Julia
Jared and Family
Kate
Jacob
Jasmine
Bella
Robert

May you follow God's path and live the adventure.

TABLE OF CONTENTS

LIST OF FIGURES

LIST OF TABLES

INTRODUCTION

*T*his book has been some twenty years in the making. Not twenty years of constant work but twenty years of spiritual growth and insight into the Word. This work was also interrupted by my work on earlier books, *Strong and Courageous* and *Walls and Gates*. In the beginning, my working title for this book was *Living the Adventure*, that is, the adventure of the Christian life. Then there was a major change in thought and content as I began to wrestle with the difference between "being in Christ" and "Christ in me." From there, I began to develop a passion for seeing believers break free from the mistaken belief that serving the Lord is something they must do by relying on their own wisdom and strength. Over the years, I have become increasingly burdened as I observe believers who attempt to live life thinking they must do the work of correcting inappropriate thinking and behavior and advancing the kingdom of God. They fail to understand the power that is available to transform their lives and empower them to become productive members of God's family.

There are many different definitions of what it means to be a Christian. For example, I am a follower of Jesus; I go to church regularly, or I am a good person. Theologian Elmer Towns suggests that for some, being a Christian means agreeing to a creed or doctrinal statement. In these cases, there is a belief in the existence of God, but one does not experience a personal relationship with the Lord or have an awareness of the active presence of the Lord in their lives.[1] Others accept a living God who is active and available to lead them through life. Still others have an abiding, personal relationship with the Lord and a faith that motivates them to be actively engaged in advancing the kingdom of God.

My purpose in this work is to describe the Christian life in terms of a spiritual journey. This journey takes one from a self-centered life without God to a productive life that empowers the Christian to make a difference in the lives of others. It is a journey from a self-seeking life to discipleship. It is a journey directed by the Holy Spirit. Discipleship is, as Eugene Peterson put it, "a long obedience in the same direction."[2] Discipleship means knowing God's plan for your life, your spiritual gifts, and the power within to carry out that plan. This journey will be described in terms of the work of the Spirit to achieve that plan.

- The spiritual journey begins at the point when a person recognizes at a deeply personal level that they need to be rescued from spiritual death and decide to trust that God will rescue them. It is the Spirit who leads one to salvation.
- The journey continues when the individual, rescued from death, becomes aware that God offers more than deliverance; he offers a rich, abundant life obtained by giving Jesus Christ control over one's life. It is the Spirit who leads one to commitment to Christ.
- For many, the journey takes on a new dimension when the believer understands that the Lord has empowered them with wisdom, strength, and motivation beyond their own abilities. It is the Spirit who leads one to a deeper life.
- Another important step in the journey involves being aware of and applying the spiritual gifts God has given and knowing that he can carry out God's calling. It means an intentional availability to be used by the Lord. It is the Father, Son, and Holy Spirit who equips believers for the work of service.

- Finally, the believer becomes a productive member of God's kingdom by unleashing the Spirit's power to lead others to the Lord and encouraging their spiritual growth. It is the Spirit who empowers believers for the work of service.

The challenge on this journey is to move from rational, human thinking that keeps us from the abundant life to living under the transforming power and influence of the Spirit enabling us to touch the lives of those he has placed on our path. I pray that you will set aside the reality of the world for the reality of life in Christ and experience the productivity and rich blessings that come from total surrender to the Lord.

Along the way, I will share my spiritual journey and provide examples that illustrate scriptural truths that are foundational to empowered living.

The Decision

ENTERING CHRIST

Jesus replied, "I tell you the truth, unless you are born again, you cannot see the Kingdom of God. I assure you, no one can enter the Kingdom of God without being born of water and the Spirit... For this is how God loved the world: He gave his one and only Son, so that everyone who believes in him will not perish but have eternal life" (John 3:3, 5, 16).

WE HAVE BEEN CREATED TO LIVE FOREVER

There is a starting point with any journey. For the Christian, that starting point is salvation. It is the understanding that we cannot live the life we want, let alone the life God calls us to live. This understanding, in whatever form it comes, leads to an intentional decision to accept God's offer of salvation through his Son, Jesus Christ. It is God's desire that all make that decision, establish a personal relationship with him, experience his power available to them, and exercise that power to advance his kingdom. With that decision, we meet the eternal God and become a part of his eternal kingdom.

God is Eternal.

By his very nature, God is eternal. "Before the mountains were born you brought forth the earth and the world, from everlasting to everlasting you are God" (Ps. 90:2). Genesis 1:1 states: "In the beginning, God..." indicating God's preexistence at creation. When Moses asked God to identify himself at the burning bush, he said, "I Am Who I Am. Say this to the people of Israel: I Am has sent me to you." God also said to Moses, "Say this to the people of Israel: Yahweh, the God of your ancestors—the God of Abraham, the God of Isaac, and the God of Jacob—has sent me to you. This is my eternal name, my name to remember for all generations" (Exod. 3:14-15). In other words, God exists in the now. Recall that Jesus, teaching in the temple, told his listeners, "Truly, truly, I say to you, before Abraham was, I am" (John 8:58). For God, there is no time or space. For God, it is always now.

We Have Been Created to Live Eternally

When God created man, he said, "Let us make man in our image, after our likeness. And let them have dominion over the fish of the sea and over the birds of the heavens and over the livestock and over all the earth and over every creeping thing that creeps on the earth" (Gen. 1:26). Being created in his image, we will live forever; we are eternal beings. God's plan for Adam and Eve was a never-ending life.[3] When God placed Adam and Eve in the garden, he warned them, "You may surely eat of every tree of the garden, but of the tree of the knowledge of good and evil you shall not eat, for in the day that you eat of it you shall surely die" (Gen. 2:15–17). This is the first mention of death. God intended for man to live forever.

Mankind Was Created to Have Fellowship with God

Scripture does not describe the nature or quality of the relationship Adam and Eve enjoyed with God. There was nothing by which to compare it. It was normal. It was natural. It was perfect, positive, and unending.

The instruction not to eat of the fruit from the tree of the knowledge of good and evil was for their benefit. It was to protect them. It was an expression of God's love. When Adam and Eve ate the forbidden fruit, their relationship with God was broken. And that gives us insight into the quality of their relationship with God. "And they heard the sound of the Lord God walking in the garden in the cool of the day, and the man and his wife hid themselves from the presence of the Lord God among the trees of the garden" (Gen. 3:8). With disobedience came fear. They were afraid of God.

Does the concept that you will live forever bring you joy or sorrow?

Being In Christ: All Fear Of Death Is Gone.

THE RELATIONSHIP DESTROYED

> The Lord God took the man and put him in the garden of Eden to work it and keep it. And the Lord God commanded the man, saying, "You may surely eat of every tree of the garden, but of the tree of the knowledge of good and evil you shall not eat, for in the day that you eat of it you shall surely die (Gen. 2:15–17).

With disobedience came death. The Hebrew word for death is *tā mūt mo-wt,* meaning "dying you shall die." [4] Our first thought is physical death: our breathing, heart, and brain activity stop. As a result of Adam and Eve's sin, we all, at some point in time, will die physically. However, physical death is a process of decline over time. Physical death did not come immediately for Adam and Eve. But, the Lord said, "In the day you eat of it you shall surely die," meaning that upon sinning, we will immediately be separated from God; a spiritual death. Because of the fall, our physical life comes with pain, suffering, conflict, and decline. All of this reminds us of our separation from God, our mortality.

For Adam and Eve, separation from God was immediate. He evicted them from the garden. They were banished from the peaceful, harmonious relationship they had with him. They had been given a choice; obedience or disobedience; live or die. They chose disobedience and death.[4]

The choice, while there is still breath in us, is to live eternally in the presence of God or, upon physical death, live eternally in the fires of hell, fires that burn continually but do not consume.

> And I saw the dead, great and small, standing before the throne, and books were opened. Then another book was opened, which is the Book of Life. And the dead were judged by what was written in the books, according to what they had done. And the sea gave up the dead who were in it, Death and Hades gave up the dead who were in them, and they were judged, each one of them, according to what they had done. Then Death and Hades were thrown into the lake of fire. This is the second death, the lake of fire. And if anyone's name was not found written in the Book of Life, he was thrown into the lake of fire (Rev. 20:12–15).

In the above verses, Jesus talks about hell being the second death, a death that follows physical death. We are given a choice, be born twice (physically and spiritually) and die once (physically), or be born once and die twice (physically and spiritually).

Jesus emphasized that the fires of hell would never go out.

> And if your hand causes you to sin, cut it off. It is better for you to enter life crippled than with two hands to go to hell, to the unquenchable fire. And if your foot causes you to sin, cut it off. It is better for you to enter life lame than with two feet to be thrown into hell. And if your eye causes you to sin, tear it out. It is better for you to enter the kingdom of God with one eye than with two eyes to be thrown into hell, "where their worm does not die and the fire is not quenched" (Mark 9:43–48).

"Then the Lord God said, 'Look, the human beings

have become like us, knowing both good and evil.
What if they reach out, take fruit from the tree of life,
and eat it? Then they will live forever!'" (Gen. 3:22–23).

When man fell, that is, when he ate of the forbidden fruit, he had knowledge of good and evil but was no longer with God. The joy of living came from "being with God" and enjoying his presence.

> Contrast this with what David said: "You make known to me the path of life; in your presence, there is fullness of joy; at your right hand are pleasures forevermore" (Ps. 16:11).[5]

When we are separated from God, we groan with the nagging thought that there is something far better. This is because death is the opposite of life, so we are driven to find ways to escape death. That is why the fertility god of the Canaanites was such a magnet for the children of Israel.[6] We are constantly seeking something to fill the void. That is why we so easily fall victim to the pressures and pleasures of the world: power, prestige, position, possessions, and the like. Contentment eludes us.

Upon eating the fruit of the tree of the knowledge of good and evil, Adam and Eve recognized two things. First, the perfect and continuing relationship with God had been destroyed. They were afraid of God; fear entered in, and they hid. The basis of fear in man is having to face a holy God and the uncertainty over impending death. Second, they were naked and ashamed—the relationship between Adam and Eve changed. The focus of each turned inward to themselves. Each saw themselves as having failed.

Do you know where you will spend eternity?

The broken relationship begs for restoration.

5

THE RELATIONSHIP RESTORED

> "I will put enmity between you and the woman, and between your offspring and her offspring; he shall bruise your head, and you shall bruise his heel" (Gen. 3:15).

With the fall, death entered the human experience. However, the Lord promised that from the offspring of the woman would come one who would rescue us from death. He would give us access to eternal life, restore fellowship with God, and provide abundant life in the present.[7]

> "Then the eyes of both were opened, and they knew that they were naked. And they sewed fig leaves together and made themselves loincloths. And the Lord God made for Adam and for his wife garments of skins and clothed them" (Gen. 3:7, 21).

Adam and Eve's attempt to solve the problem of their nakedness failed. Due to the sin of Adam and Eve, we search for redemption through any other means than through the sacrifice of the "seed" of the woman, Jesus Christ. Only God can adequately cover our sins. The Lord covered the nakedness of Adam and Eve with animal skins. He covered the shame they felt as a result of their sin. To do that, the Lord had to kill animals. He sacrificed animals to cover their sin. Clearly, this foreshadowed the death of Christ on the cross and the shedding of his blood to cover our sins. Our relationship with God can only be restored through the death of Christ. Only then can we have eternal life. Only then are we rescued from the unquenchable fires of hell?

Also, recall that the Lord reinforced the importance of the shedding of blood to protect the children of Israel from the angel of death in Egypt. The blood had to be from an unblemished lamb and placed on the doorposts and lintel (beam over the door) of their homes in Egypt. That blood was a covering (Exod. 12:1–11).

Moreover, Adam and Eve were fired from their job of guarding the Tree of Life. They were replaced by cherubim (Gen. 3:24). The Lord instructed Moses to place images of cherubim over the ark of the covenant, over the presence of the Lord (Exod. 25:18–22).

From the beginning, God's plan was to provide a way for us to be reconciled with him, to live in a restored relationship with Him. That plan was through the shedding of blood, through a sacrifice. That ritual of sacrifice continued down through the centuries, ending ultimately in Christ's death on the cross. With Christ's death, the need for a sacrificial system ended. He died once for all (Heb. 7:27; 9:26; 10:10).

The redemption of Adam and Eve is implied rather than explicit. In fact, the word redemption or redeemed does not appear in the story of the creation and fall. The first appearance of the word (chronologically) in Scripture is in Job.

> "For I know that my Redeemer lives, and at the last he will stand upon the earth. And after my skin has been thus destroyed, yet in my flesh I shall see God, whom I shall see for myself, and my eyes shall behold, and not another. My heart faints within me!" (Job 19:25–27).

Clearly, Job understood redemption. The fact that he knew that his Redeemer lived indicates a profound understanding that he needed redemption. The Hebrew word for redeemer is *go 'al*, which is frequently referred to as a kinsman-redeemer. In legal terms, the kinsman-redeemer had rights and responsibilities to buy back or restore a family member to freedom. *Go 'al* clearly establishes that there is a relationship between the one who is in bondage and the one doing the rescuing.[8] In one of the great statements of faith in Scripture, Job rested in the belief that his Redeemer was God himself and that he, Job, was a part of God's family.

We have been created by God, and therefore we are his children. Like Job, we can depend on God to rescue us from slavery, bondage, and captivity. Our disobedience alienates us from God. There is nothing we can do to restore that relationship. Therefore, God stepped in to break the bonds that hold us captive, bonds that separate us from him.

The patriarch Jacob, in blessing his sons on his deathbed,

recognized God as his Kinsman-Redeemer:

> "And he blessed Joseph and said, "The God before whom my fathers Abraham and Isaac walked, the God who has been my shepherd all my life long to this day, the angel who has redeemed me from all evil . . ." (Gen. 48:15–16).

We are redeemed when we recognize, as did Adam and Eve, Jacob, Job, and others of the Old Testament, that we need a kinsman-redeemer. God, through Christ, is our Kinsman Redeemer. Redemption comes when we personally accept the sacrifice of Christ on the cross. When we do that, we enter Christ, and he covers us from the wrath of God. "There is therefore now no condemnation for those who are in Christ Jesus" (Rom. 8:1).

Do you know that God has covered your faults and failures?

Being in Christ: My relationship with God is restored.

GROANING

> To the woman he said, "I will surely multiply your pain in childbearing; in pain you shall bring forth children. Your desire shall be contrary to your husband, but he shall rule over you." And to Adam he said, "Because you have listened to the voice of your wife and have eaten of the tree of which I commanded you, 'You shall not eat of it,' cursed is the ground because of you; in pain you shall eat of it all the days of your life; thorns and thistles it shall bring forth for you; and you shall eat the plants of the field. By the sweat of your face you shall eat bread, till you return to the ground, for out of it you were taken; for you are dust, and to dust you shall return" (Gen. 3:16–19).

Without redemption, we are destined to groan in life. Note that the promise of redemption comes before the promise of toil, trials, and turmoil. We sense there is something better than the present life. The dictionary describes a groan as the voicing of a deep, unarticulated sound, as of pain, grief, or displeasure. It is to make a sound expressing stress or strain.[9] Groaning is different from grumbling. While groaning is a reaction when we cannot do anything about our situation, grumbling is what we do when things do not go as expected. We will focus on groaning here and grumbling later.

Scripture describes groaning in two situations. First is the burden of grief:

> "I am feeble and crushed; I groan because of the tumult of my heart" (Ps. 38:8).

> "When the righteous increase, the people rejoice, but when the wicked rule, the people groan" (Prov. 29:2).

The second aspect of groaning in Scripture is an inward expression by those who live in the hope of glory, awaiting the translation of our earthly bodies into the eternal presence of the Lord. It has been said that biblical hope is the excited anticipation of an assured thing.

> "And not only the creation, but we, who have the first fruits of the Spirit, groan inwardly as we wait eagerly for adoption as sons, the redemption of our bodies" (Rom. 8:23).

> For we know that if the tent that is our earthly home is destroyed, we have a building from God, a house not made with hands, eternal in the heavens. For in this tent we groan, longing to put on our heavenly dwelling, if indeed by putting it on we may not be found naked. For while we are still in this tent, we groan, being burdened—not that we would be unclothed, but that we would be further clothed, so that what is mortal may be swallowed up by life (2 Cor. 5:1–4).

Groaning in the Old Testament

The children of Jacob spent 430 years in Egypt. They were slaves to the Egyptians whose treatment of the people became increasingly harsh.

> "So they ruthlessly made the people of Israel work as slaves and made their lives bitter with hard service, in mortar and brick, and in all kinds of work in the field. In all their work they ruthlessly made them work as slaves" (Exod. 1:13–14).

The Hebrews asked for time to go away to sacrifice to the Lord. Pharaoh responded by demanding that they make bricks without straw and produce the same number of bricks as in the past. There was groaning throughout the land (Exod. 5:15–23).

Israel groaned under the oppression of the Egyptians. They cried out to God, and God responded. He rescued them. He delivered them from death. He saved them. In doing so, he kept his promise to Abram that he would deliver them. He created a way of escape from Pharaoh's pursuing army and death.

> "But the people of Israel walked on dry ground through the sea, the waters being a wall to them on their right hand and on their left. Thus the Lord saved Israel that day from the hand of the Egyptians, and Israel saw the Egyptians dead on the seashore" (Exod. 14:29–30).

Groaning in the New Testament

> Now there was a man of the Pharisees named Nicodemus, a ruler of the Jews. This man came to Jesus by night and said to him, "Rabbi, we know that you are a teacher come from God, for no one can do these signs that you do unless God is with him." Jesus answered him, "Truly, truly, I say to you, unless one is born again he cannot see the kingdom of God" (John 3:1–3).

As a ruler of the Jews, we can conclude that Nicodemus was a wise and good man. He had power, position, and prestige. He knew the law and the prophets by heart. Upon seeing Jesus's miracles and hearing him teach, he developed a nagging doubt about his eternal destiny. Notice that he came to Jesus at night. Some suggest that he was afraid of being seen with Jesus. Others suggest he wanted one-on-one time with Jesus, time he could not get in the crowds during the day. Perhaps there is a third alternative; Nicodemus was living in darkness. Darkness and light are constant themes in John's writing. It was spiritual uncertainty that brought Nicodemus to Jesus.

He was seeking to resolve the emptiness he was experiencing. His spirit was groaning. The spirit of fallen man groans continually as it seeks release from the sense of futility. Nicodemus's nighttime appearance implies the question: Is this all there is?

Moreover, he thought he had done everything needed to satisfy God. He went through all the motions required by the Law. Yet, he did not recognize that it was the condition of his heart that mattered to God. Nicodemus had a spiritual problem. The Messiah came to offer a spiritual solution, not a human solution. We will deal with Jesus's conversation with Nicodemus in more detail later.

What caused the groaning of the Israelites, Nicodemus, and those listening to Jesus? The people were under control of Roman authorities. But there is a deeper, more significant reason for their groaning. It is the fallen nature of man, separation from God, and man's inability to restore that relationship on his own. It is emptiness. "There is a way that seems right to a man, but its end is the way to death" (Prov. 14:12). There is a natural desire to follow our own methods and desires.

It is in our DNA to disobey, to sin and then groan at our failure.

> "And this is the judgment: the light has come into the world, and people loved the darkness rather than the light because their works were evil. For everyone who does wicked things hates the light and does not come to the light, lest his works should be exposed" (John 3:19–20).

Another example of groaning in the New Testament is the

people's response to the preaching of Peter, first in Acts 2 when Peter was preaching to the crowd at Pentecost:

> "Let all the house of Israel therefore know for certain that God has made him both Lord and Christ, this Jesus whom you crucified." Now when they heard this they were cut to the heart, and said to Peter and the rest of the apostles, "Brothers, what shall we do?" And Peter said to them, "Repent and be baptized every one of you in the name of Jesus Christ for the forgiveness of your sins, and you will receive the gift of the Holy Spirit. For the promise is for you and for your children and for all who are far off, everyone whom the Lord our God calls to himself" (Acts 2:36–39).

And again, in Acts chapter 3, when Peter preached to the Jews at the Temple:

> "And now, brothers, I know that you acted in ignorance, as did also your rulers. But what God foretold by the mouth of all the prophets, that his Christ would suffer, he thus fulfilled. Repent therefore, and turn back, that your sins may be blotted out" (Acts 3:17–19).

Notice the groaning of the people in their response to Peter: "What shall we do?" Peter's reply was: "Repent and be converted."

Scripture is clear that salvation is found in no one except Jesus Christ.

> So Jesus again said to them, "Truly, truly, I say to you, I am the door of the sheep. All who came before me are thieves and robbers, but the sheep did not listen to them. I am the door. If anyone enters by me, he will be saved and will go in and out and find pasture. The thief comes only to steal and kill and destroy. I came that they may have life and have it abundantly" (John 10:7–9).

Jesus said to her, "I am the resurrection and the life. Whoever believes in me, though he die, yet shall he

live, and everyone who lives and believes in me shall never die. Do you believe this?" (John 11:25–26).

Jesus said to him, "I am the way, and the truth, and the life. No one comes to the Father except through me" (John 14:6).

"This Jesus is the stone that was rejected by you, the builders, which has become the cornerstone. And there is salvation in no one else, for there is no other name under heaven given among men by which we must be saved" (Acts 4:11–12).

Do you sense that there is something better? Have you found peace with God?

Being in Christ: I am eternally satisfied.

CONFESSION AND REPENTANCE

"If we say we have no sin, we deceive ourselves, and the truth is not in us. If we confess our sins, he is faithful and just to forgive us our sins and to cleanse us from all unrighteousness. If we say we have not sinned, we make him a liar, and his word is not in us" (1 John 1:8–10).

To confess (*Homologes* in the Greek) means to recognize God's character and work and acknowledge one's sin. It is to accept or agree that he is God, and we are not. Confession is an acknowledgment of one's position with respect to God, an agreement with a charge being brought, an expression of a deep conviction, a recognition of God's saving acts in history, and a statement representing a change of conviction. The opposite of confess is to deny.[10]

To repent (*Mateoasate* in the Greek) means to change one's mind for better; to alter course with remorse for one's past sins; to consciously alter one's attitude, will, purpose, and the direction of one's life because of the conviction of sin. Repenting is the recognition that God is right, and we are wrong. It is turning away from, abandoning, or repudiating a disobedient lifestyle. It is a conscious, moral separation or putting behind. It is an inward, conscious decision based on a conviction that our ways are evil, and we need to leave those attitudes, behavior, or thoughts behind. It is also a commitment to move away from self-centered actions. Repenting is an action required to receive forgiveness from God or others. "In those days John the Baptist came preaching in the wilderness of Judea, "Repent, for the kingdom of heaven is at hand"" (Matt. 3:1–2). Peter, in his exhortation at Pentecost, called his audience to recognize the pending judgment over their disobedience and turn their back on it.[11]

Peter's sermon was not just to the Jews but to all mankind. Repentance covers all failures in all peoples, places, and cultures. Peter's call was for his audience (us) to change their (our) mind about Jesus. This is what Paul preached to the Athenians: "The times of ignorance God overlooked, but now he commands all people everywhere to repent, because he has fixed a day on which he will judge the world in righteousness by a man whom he has appointed; and of this he has given assurance to all by raising him from the dead" (Acts 17:30–31). Jesus is more than a historical figure, teacher, or martyr. He died to offer us eternal life and access to the throne of God.

> John the Baptist preached repentance in preparation for the coming Messiah; he preached repentance as a prerequisite for salvation. "From that time Jesus began to preach, saying, 'Repent, for the kingdom of heaven is at hand'" (Matt. 4:17).

Both Judas and Peter sinned as Jesus moved resolutely toward the cross. Note the difference in their response to their sin. When Judas saw that Jesus was condemned, he had remorse for what he did. He regretted his betrayal. He attempted to rectify the situation by returning the silver to the Jewish leaders. His sin, however, was against God, not man. His remorse led to despair, hopelessness, and overwhelming guilt that led him to take his own life. His suicide is clear evidence that he did not repent or turn away from his actions. On the other hand, Peter had remorse for denying Christ. He responded by confessing and repenting, and Jesus forgave and restored him.

While prophets, preachers, and the Word call us to repentance, it is the Holy Spirit who creates the desire to repent. That is the first work of the Holy Spirit. He allows for remorse within us for our sinful lives. We, however, have a choice to either respond to the urging of the Spirit or reject it. Faith is the belief that we can be pardoned of our sin and be restored. Faith is the belief that repentance brings restoration. The author of Hebrews put it this way: "And without faith it is impossible to please him, for whoever would draw near to God must believe that he exists and that he rewards those who seek him" (Heb. 11:6). Note that we are dealing with personal trust rather than an intellectual agreement, acceptance, or mere knowledge. Repentance is an act of faith, believing that God can and will forgive us. Jesus was clear about the role of the Holy Spirit in repentance.

> Nevertheless, I tell you the truth: it is to your advantage that I go away, for if I do not go away, the Helper will not come to you. But if I go, I will send him to you. And when he comes, he will convict the world concerning sin and righteousness and judgment: concerning sin, because they do not believe in me; concerning righteousness, because I go to the Father, and you will see me no longer; concerning judgment, because the ruler of this world is judged (John 16:7–11).

Confession: admitting failure to obey the Lord, admitting we are wrong.

Repentance: the desire to turn our life away from sin and move in a new direction.

Have you confessed that he is God, and you are not? Do you have a deep desire to move in a different direction?

Being in Christ: acceptance and restoration.

JESUS'S DISCOURSE ON SALVATION

The Problem

> Now there was a man of the Pharisees named
> Nicodemus, a ruler of the Jews. This man came to
> Jesus by night and said to him, "Rabbi, we know that
> you are a teacher come from God, for no one can do
> these signs that you do unless God is with him." Jesus
> answered him, "Truly, truly, I say to you, unless one is
> born again he cannot see the kingdom of God."
> Nicodemus said to him, "How can a man be born when
> he is old? Can he enter a second time into his mother's
> womb and be born?" (John 3:1–4).

Recall that we discussed Nicodemus earlier as he sought answers to
his emptiness. Note that Jesus moved directly to Nicodemus's spiritual
condition, his need to be born again. Nicodemus was puzzled because he
was thinking in physical terms. This is typical of the other six one-on-
one conversations Jesus had with individuals recorded in John. Jesus
spoke in spiritual terms, and his listeners heard what he was saying in
physical terms.

Jesus stated that entering the family of God required being born
again. The two words "born again" in the Greek are *gennao,* which
means to arise or excite, and *anothen,* which means from above.[12]
Jesus said that one must be born from above. It is not a matter of one's
genealogy—or in Nicodemus's case, being a Jew or a Pharisee. To be
born again comes from a conscious decision to accept God's offer of
adoption into his family.

There is more to Nicodemus's question than just the physical
impossibility of re-entering his mother's womb. He was asking: "How can
a man who has lived in the world and having habits and ways of
thinking expect such a radical change?"[13] Jesus's point was that, just as
physical rebirth is not possible, neither is spiritual rebirth without
divine action. Another takeaway from this conversation is that we
dwell in the world. We deal in the physical so much that we fail to see

life in spiritual terms. Paul prayed this for the Ephesian believers:

> I do not cease to give thanks for you, remembering you
> in my prayers, that the God of our Lord Jesus Christ,
> the Father of glory, may give you the Spirit of wisdom
> and of revelation in the knowledge of him, having the
> eyes of your hearts enlightened, that you may know
> what is the hope to which he has called you, what are the
> riches of his glorious inheritance in the saints (Eph.
> 1:16–18).

Jesus said that for one to see spiritually, one had to be born from above. Understanding spiritual things flows out of a spiritual birth. There are two types of people in the world: those who are spiritually confused and those who are not. Nicodemus was confused.

The Spirit

> "Jesus answered, "Truly, truly, I say to you, unless one
> is born of water and the Spirit, he cannot enter the
> kingdom of God. That which is born of the flesh is
> flesh, and that which is born of the Spirit is spirit. Do
> not marvel that I said to you, 'You must be born again'"
> (John 3:5–7).

Jesus said the requirement to enter the kingdom is to be born of water and the Spirit. Water represents cleansing. It is symbolic of the Spirit and baptism. Some speculate that Jesus was referring to John the Baptist who preached repentance and baptism for cleansing.[14] Jesus said that one must be drawn to salvation by the Spirit. Later he said that the role of the Holy Spirit was to convict of sin, righteousness, and judgment (John 16:7-11). Spiritual birth involves cleansing and transformation.

Jesus challenged Nicodemus's thinking. As a Pharisee, he focused on outward appearances and was legalistic in his judgment. Moreover, proselytes to Judaism were immersed in water to symbolically wash away the impurities of idolatry. They were also given new clothing. This did not apply to the Jews—they were already under the covenant.

They were sons of Abraham and children of God from birth. However, having descended from Abraham was not sufficient for salvation. Jesus was saying: Everyone must repent individually and begin a new life.[15] What Jesus said in verse 7 was: You (singular) should know these things because you are a teacher of the Law. Jesus continued by saying, "You (plural—everyone) must be born again." For example:

> I will take you from the nations and gather you from all the countries and bring you into your own land. I will sprinkle clean water on you, and you shall be clean from all your uncleannesses, and from all your idols I will cleanse you. And I will give you a new heart, and a new spirit I will put within you. And I will remove the heart of stone from your flesh and give you a heart of flesh. And I will put my Spirit within you, and cause you to walk in my statutes and be careful to obey my rules. You shall dwell in the land that I gave to your fathers, and you shall be my people, and I will be your God (Ezek. 36:25–28).

> Jesus continued: "The wind blows where it wishes, and you hear its sound, but you do not know where it comes from or where it goes. So it is with everyone who is born of the Spirit" (John 3:8).

We know neither the origin nor destination of the wind, but it is observable and real. We cannot see the wind, but we can feel it and see its effects. Today we understand that wind is produced by a change in atmospheric pressure. Regardless, the analogy holds. The work of the Spirit drawing us to salvation is mysterious though observable. In the Greek, wind and spirit are the same word, *pneuma*.[16]

The conversation continued.

> Nicodemus said to him, "How can these things be?" Jesus answered him, "Are you the teacher of Israel and yet you do not understand these things? Truly, truly, I

say to you, we speak of what we know, and bear witness to what we have seen, but you do not receive our testimony. If I have told you earthly things and you do not believe, how can you believe if I tell you heavenly things? No one has ascended into heaven except he who descended from heaven, the Son of Man. And as Moses lifted up the serpent in the wilderness, so must the Son of Man be lifted up, that whoever believes in him may have eternal life" (John 3:9–15).

Jesus continued to challenge Nicodemus: "How could you not know or understand this?" Jesus needed to shake Nicodemus out of his firm but incorrect thinking. Moreover, Jesus said that the method for receiving salvation was no different from that preached by the prophets. It is by revelation, not discovery, that one comes to faith. In other words, if you do not grasp what you have been taught, how can you expect to understand the deeper things of the Spirit.

Jesus continued by drawing a parallel between himself and an event in the Old Testament (Num. 21:8–9), where God provided the antidote for snake venom. Israel was disobedient and God sent poisonous snakes as judgment. The people had no escape. There was no antidote for the poison. God instructed Moses to elevate a bronze serpent. When the people looked up to the serpent they were healed. Jesus told Nicodemus that he, Jesus, would be "lifted up" for the sins of man, and by believing men would be saved. By accepting Jesus's sacrifice on the cross one can be saved. The blood shed by Jesus on the cross is the antidote for sin.

Belief

"For God so loved the world that He gave His only begotten Son, that whoever believes in Him should not perish but have everlasting life. For God did not send His Son into the world to condemn the world, but that the world through Him might be saved" (John 3:16–18 NKJV).

There is an interesting transition in tense within these verses. Jesus began in the past tense (loved, gave, sent, saved) and then moved into the present tense (perish, have, believes). Author, Gene Edwards, reflecting on "the Lamb that was slain at the creation of the world (Rev 13:8)," describes Jesus as having nail holes in his hands and feet and the wound in his side before the beginning.[17] God does not live in time or space. He has already acted. What is past is present. But we live in both time and space. Therefore, it is important to believe (present tense) and be saved (past tense).

Jesus emphasized love, not condemnation. From the fall onward, God has been aggressively pursuing rebellious man, not to punish him but to restore him to a right relationship with him. It is his great desire that none perish but for all to come to repentance (2 Pe 3:9).

Jesus said that those who believe "shall not perish" (NKJV). In the Greek, the word for perish is *apollumi.* It means the opposite of life—to die, to be hopelessly alienated from God, to exist in eternal judgment. It also carries the idea of being lost (existing but not being present) and, therefore, useless, such as an old wineskin that will not hold new wine or spoiled fruit. To perish conveys the idea of utter futility.[17]

Jesus promised "everlasting life." The Greek uses two words: *aionios,* meaning without beginning or end, and *zoe,* meaning physical and spiritual life—both coming from God.[18] By sending Jesus to die in our place, God made the ultimate sacrifice so that we could enjoy eternal fellowship with him.

Jesus identified himself as *shaliach,* the Jewish concept of the messenger, the one who is sent and who, in turn, sends, the one who is commissioned and faithfully carries out the plan of the sender.[19]

Note that God changes the object of his salvation from his historic love for Israel to his love for the world. God sacrificed his only Son for every person from Adam onward (John 3:16).

Salvation is a gift from God. To be saved, one must believe that God's offer of salvation is individual and personal and then accept that gift. One is either a believer or not. One is either saved or destined for eternal damnation. There can be no greater love than that expressed by Jesus on the cross for all rebellious men.

Have you been born again—born from above?

Being in Christ: I will not perish.

BEING IN CHRIST

"But now that you have been set free from sin and have become slaves of God, the fruit you get leads to sanctification and its end, eternal life. For the wages of sin is death, but the free gift of God is eternal life **in Christ Jesus** our Lord" (Rom. 6:22–23, emphasis added).

"There is therefore now no condemnation for those who are in Christ Jesus. For the law of the Spirit of life has set you free **in Christ Jesus** from the law of sin and death" (Rom. 8:1–2, emphasis added).

"For as in Adam all die, so also **in Christ** shall all be made alive" (1 Cor. 15:22, emphasis added).

"Remember that you were at that time separated from Christ, alienated from the commonwealth of Israel and strangers to the covenants of promise, having no hope and without God in the world. But now **in Christ Jesus** you who once were far off have been brought near by the blood of Christ" (Eph. 2:12–13, emphasis added).

From the eviction of Adam and Eve from the garden, man had groaned over his inability to deal with separation from God and his impending death. Repentance changes our position with respect to God and death. When we repent, it places us positionally *in Christ*. We are hidden in Christ. Since we have sinned and continue to sin, being in Christ prevents God's wrath from dealing with us as we deserve.

In the above passages, Paul makes the distinction between those who are "in Christ" and those who are not. Being in Christ is to be fully alive. To be "in Christ" means we are under the protective covering of the perfect Christ. God does not allow sin in his presence. Therefore, God will not allow anyone into his presence **unless** they come to him "in Christ." It means we have died with Christ, been buried with Christ, and been resurrected with Christ. When God looks at us, he only sees Christ, his perfect Son.

Have you chosen to live eternally in the presence of God?

Being in Christ: experiencing the eternal presence of God.

WHY DO PEOPLE REJECT THE OFFER OF SALVATION

"But God shows his love for us in that while we were still sinners, Christ died for us. Since, therefore, we have now been justified by his blood, much more shall we be saved by him from the wrath of God" (Rom. 5:8–9).

"But God, being rich in mercy, because of the great love with which he loved us, even when we were dead in our trespasses, made us alive together with Christ— by grace you have been saved—and raised us up with him and seated us with him in the heavenly places in Christ Jesus..." (Eph. 2:4–6).

"For as by a man came death, by a man has come also the resurrection of the dead. For as in Adam all die, so also in Christ shall all be made alive" (1 Cor. 15:21–22).

It is the Holy Spirit who leads us to the throne of grace. While we are branded with the sin of Adam, God provided the solution: the personal acceptance of Christ's death on the cross, and salvation.

On April 14, 1912, the RMS *Titanic* hit an iceberg and began sinking. "Those aboard *Titanic* were ill-prepared for such an emergency... The crew had not been trained adequately in carrying out an evacuation. The officers did not know how many they could safely put aboard the lifeboats and launched many of them barely half-full. Third-class passengers were largely left to fend for themselves, causing many of them to become trapped below deck as the ship filled with water."[20] Consider this from a spiritual perspective:

- The *Titanic* was thought to be unsinkable. Life goes on in the belief that nothing bad will happen.
- The officers were not prepared for such a disaster. Not all churches are prepared to rescue people floundering in unbelief.
- Many lifeboats were launched only half-full. Many who come to our churches are not led to repentance and rescue.
- Third-class passengers were left on their own, many below deck. We ignore those who are not like us.

A friend enrolled in an Evangelism Explosion class. As a first step, he was asked to identify areas of his life that would hinder his leading others to Christ. He made the list and was reminded that the Lord had already covered his sins. He was then instructed to burn the list as a symbol of the Lord's forgiveness. He did that but, upon returning the next week, confessed that, despite burning the list, he was still burdened by what was on the list. The leader, recognizing the problem, led him in a prayer for salvation, and the burden of guilt was gone.

Through repentance, we are presented to God the Father, perfect in Christ.

Why do people fail to accept the offer of salvation?

- They are ignorant. They are not aware that they need salvation or do not know how to receive salvation.
- They love sin. Salvation is a threat to the life they love.
- They reject the idea of giving up something they see for something they cannot see.
- They consider it to be inconvenient at the time. They can always do it later.

After the collapse of the twin towers on September 11, 2001, there were many public comments about the loss of innocent life. On the following Sunday a pastor entitled his Sunday message "There are no innocent people... for all have sinned and fall short of the glory of God" (Rom. 3:23).

God Actively Seeks Us

We sin. Try as we might, we cannot escape the penalty of death. The good news is that God does not want us to continue in that state. He actively works to bring us under the saving grace of Christ.

> "And they heard the sound of the Lord God walking in the garden in the cool of the day, and the man and his wife hid themselves from the presence of the Lord God among the trees of the garden. But the Lord God called to the man and said to him, 'Where are you?'" (Gen. 3:8–9).

> What man of you, having a hundred sheep, if he has lost one of them, does not leave the ninety-nine in the open country, and go after the one that is lost, until he finds it? And when he has found it, he lays it on his shoulders, rejoicing. And when he comes home, he calls together his friends and his neighbors, saying to them, "Rejoice with me, for I have found my sheep that was lost." Just so, I tell you, there will be more joy in heaven over one sinner who repents than over ninety-nine righteous persons who need no repentance (Luke 15:4–7).

> "This is good, and it is pleasing in the sight of God our Savior, who desires all people to be saved and to come to the knowledge of the truth" (1 Tim. 2:3–4).

We sin because we are descendants of Adam and Eve. It is in our nature, our DNA. We also resist God's efforts to redeem us. However, God has laid out the path to bring us into his family. We have a choice. We can respond to his call, or we can reject it.

Do you know someone who is groaning because they cannot fix the problem of their sin?

Are you avoiding the issue of life everlasting; are you putting that decision off?

Being in Christ: the problem of sin resolved.

PEACE WITH GOD

From a biblical perspective, peace means "to be complete" or "to be sound." Peace comes from the Hebrew word *shalom*. *Shalom* also means having a right relationship between two parties, with each other, but more importantly with God. Because of the fall, the relationship with God must be restored. This restoration happens with confession, acknowledging to God that we are sinners and need salvation. It is a confession that God is right, and we are wrong; that we are in conflict with God in our thoughts, attitudes, and behaviors. Only by accepting God's offer of salvation can our relationship with God be restored, and we can begin living in his presence. Only then can we begin living in righteous harmony with God.[21]

> "In peace I will both lie down and sleep; for you alone, O Lord, make me dwell in safety" (Ps. 4:8).

> "Great peace have those who love your law; nothing can make them stumble" (Ps. 119:165).

> Peace is a calm heart for those who trust God. Peace is the outcome for those who sincerely seek the Lord.

> "Turn away from evil and do good; seek peace and pursue it" (Ps. 34:14).

The word for peace in the Greek is *eirene*. Its meaning evolved over time until it paralleled that of Hebrew tradition. The gospel clearly states that the primary need of man is peace with God, which is available only through Jesus Christ. He is the Prince of Peace. He is our peace (Eph. 2:14). Joseph Henry Thayer, the nineteenth-century biblical scholar, defined peace as "a conception distinctly peculiar to Christianity, the tranquil state of a soul assured of its salvation through Christ. And so fearing nothing from God."[22]

Peace with God is not to be confused with the peace of God. Peace of God is a benefit of making Jesus the Lord of our life. We will cover this in the next chapter. Peace with God comes only when our war with God is over. It comes when we acknowledge that he is God, and we are not. Have you accepted Jesus Christ as your savior?

Being in Christ: The war is over; there is peace at last.

MY JOURNEY TO SALVATION

Some of us may wish that God has grandchildren and, by virtue of our genealogy, automatically gain admission to heaven. Quite the opposite is true. Our heritage is from Adam, and we are born sinners. Having descended from Adam, I was separated from God at birth. I needed salvation. I needed a kinsman-redeemer. I had to come to him on a personal basis, not because of my genes, heritage, or culture.

In English village churchyards, there are grave markers for Tripp men. Several of those markers bear the prefix "Rev." My Grandfather and his brothers were lay preachers in the Methodist church. My cousin, Dorothy, was a medical missionary in Hyderabad, India, for nearly thirty years. My cousin, David Tripp, grew up under the mentoring of our grandfather and became a pastor in the Methodist church. My father, on the other hand, took a detour for many years. It may have started when he immigrated to the US and became involved with a pseudo-religious, works-oriented organization. Over the years, I had several conversations with him about his eternal destiny. He was certain that he would get to heaven because of his good, moral life and service to others. In our discussions, his thoughts on salvation reflected the belief system of the men with whom he associated. He somehow missed the good news that we cannot earn our place in heaven and that salvation is only offered to us as a gift.

At age ninety-one, confronted by his own mortality and troubled by Jesus's statement that not everyone who said "Lord, Lord" would enter the kingdom of God (Matt. 7:21), he accepted Christ as his Savior. In a subsequent conversation, I asked him what he thought his spiritual gift was. He said, "The gift of salvation." That answer was not from anything we had discussed. It was from the Holy Spirit. He was assured of his salvation. My parents were very involved in their church, and I attended with them whether I wanted to or not. I have vivid memories of Sunday school teachers and others in the church who lived lives that were distinctly different from others, both inside and outside the church. In several cases, I was sure that I did not want to be like them because they were too "churchy."

During my early teens, I attended church camp each summer. I clearly recall the last evening at one of the camps. The final night involved a service around a campfire, during which I symbolically laid a stick of wood onto the fire representing what Christ did for my sins on the cross (by descending into hell). This action represented repentance. I did not understand it in those terms at the time. However, it was my point of salvation.

Being in Christ: He found me.

When Did Your Spiritual Journey Begin?

The spiritual journey is different for each of us. We are unique individuals in the sight of God. He has very specific and individual plans for each of us. However, for each of us, that journey has a starting point: salvation. Some recall a specific time and place where that event took place. For others, awareness of that event may be uncertain. But they are aware that a change took place in their lives because of confession and repentance.

If you truly want to transfer your trust from your own devices to the saving grace of Jesus Christ, I invite you to pray this prayer.

Lord Jesus, I believe you are the Son of God. Thank you for dying on the cross for my sins. Please forgive my sins and give me the gift of eternal life. I ask you into my life and heart to be my Lord and Savior. I want to serve you always.

Have you accepted God's offer of salvation through his Son, Jesus Christ?

Being in Christ: victory over sin and death.

Empowered Living

CHRIST IN ME

Yet a little while and the world will see me no more, but you will see me. Because I live, you also will live. In that day you will know that I am in my Father, and you in me, and I in you. Whoever has my commandments and keeps them, he it is who loves me. And he who loves me will be loved by my Father, and I will love him and manifest myself to him (John 14:19–21).

There are two parts to the Christian life: the beginning (salvation—a point in time) and a journey (spiritual transformation—a lifelong process). In the above verses, Jesus was preparing his disciples for his death, burial, and resurrection, he affirmed that he and the Father were one and that his disciples were in him, and he was in them.

With salvation, we are placed firmly in Christ. We are protected from the wrath of God. Theologian Elmer Towns suggests that only a few believers understand the significance of "being in Christ" at salvation.[23]

But Jesus's message to the disciples goes a step further. He said, "I am in you." The following pages discuss the meaning of "Christ in me." Once we are alive in Christ (salvation), he is alive in us and is available to begin the process of spiritual transformation.

Do you know Christ in you?

Christ in me: empowered living.

THE EMPTINESS

"Vanity of vanities, says the Preacher, vanity of vanities! All is vanity" (Eccles. 1:2).

Seventeenth-century French philosopher, theologian, mathematician, and scientist Blasé Pascal said, "There is a God shaped vacuum in the heart of every man which cannot be filled by any created thing, but only by God, the Creator, made known through Jesus."[24]

In Pascal's day, the Catholic Church and eminent scientists denied the existence of a vacuum, claiming that such a concept denied the very existence of God. Pascal, on the other hand, filled a one-meter glass tube with mercury and inverted it into a dish of mercury. As atmospheric pressure decreased, the mercury in the tube dropped, leaving a vacuum or empty space at the top. He concluded that a vacuum does not pull in but varies according to external pressure.

Applying Pascal's experiment to the "God-shaped vacuum," we are pressured on all sides to fill the vacuum with power, position, prestige, possessions, and perfection. Scripture states that only God can fill the void in our lives. Only God can satisfy the longing in our spirit and bring meaning to life. Pascal was saying that we are created with a longing to seek after something that satisfactorily fills the God-shaped vacuum. When we do not allow God to fill that vacuum, we engage in a futile search for meaning and significance. C. S. Lewis put it another way:

> God made us: invented us as a man invents an engine. A car is made to run on petrol, and it would not run properly on anything else. Now God designed the human machine to run on Himself. He Himself is the fuel our spirits were designed to burn, or the food our spirits were designed to feed on. There is no other. That is why it is just no good asking God to make us happy in our own way without bothering about religion. God cannot give us a happiness and peace apart from Himself, because it is not there. There is no such thing.[25]

Solomon describes the futile search for meaning aside from the presence of God:

> Vanity of vanities, says the Preacher, vanity of vanities! All is vanity. What does man gain by all the toil at which he toils under the sun? A generation goes, and a generation comes, but the earth remains forever. All things are full of weariness; a man cannot utter it; the eye is not satisfied with seeing, nor the ear filled with hearing. What has been is what will be, and what has been done is what will be done, and there is nothing new under the sun (Eccles. 1:2–4, 8–9).

In my college years, I enjoyed reading novels by Ernest Hemingway. Hemingway's main characters actively sought to find meaning in life. They tried alcohol, sex, war, prizefighting, religious ritual, fishing, and big game hunting, all attempts to satisfy their deep, internal yearning for peace. His novels were exciting but empty. Hemingway's characters were in a futile search for meaning and significance as did Hemingway himself, who took his own life.

Are you running on empty, or are you experiencing the fullness of life?

Christ in me: There is no substitute.

MY DECISION

After my salvation, there was a haunting, disturbing ache in my life. I had a sense that there was something more. I continued searching. I sought answers in literature and philosophy. I was saved, but I was just going through the motions. I attended church regularly out of a sense of duty. I even taught Sunday school.

In April 1971, I attended a Lay Witness Mission. A lay witness mission involves a group of visiting laypeople spending a weekend in a church sharing their testimonies. I was invited to sit in on the team meetings.

During the preparations for the Saturday evening service, the team leader stressed that the focus that evening was on commitment. He asked if anyone present had not made a commitment to Christ. I realized that I did not have the joy that I had observed in members of the team and that I had never fully addressed the issue of my commitment to Christ. There was something in the leader's appeal that resonated with me. Things came to a halt while the team led me in a prayer of commitment.

Honestly, I did not expect any real change in my life. However, within a few days, I realized that there had been a dramatic change. For example:

- I had peace – There was no longer an emptiness in my soul. There were no longer any doubts.
- I was spending time in prayer – because I wanted to.
- I was spending time in the Word – because I wanted to.
- I saw things in familiar passages of Scripture that I had never seen before.
- I wanted to be in church—not out of a sense of duty but out of a desire to be with God's people.
- I had joy.

All of this came without conscious effort. I knew what I needed to do and proceeded without thinking. The Lord made real changes in my life. I stand in awe as I look back on my life and see how God worked:

- He gave me direct access to the throne of God.
- He brought godly people into my life to challenge and encourage me.
- He expanded my spiritual walk through good and bad experiences.
- He gave me a desire to be in the Word and opened it to me.
- He placed me in positions of ministry and encouraged me as I

saw changes in the lives of others.
- He worked to change my attitudes and behaviors.

Have you made Jesus Christ the Lord of your life?

Christ in me: filling the void.

SPIRITUAL TRANSFORMATION

"He restores my soul. He leads me in paths of righteousness for his name's sake" (Ps. 23:3).

Conversion is the process of being changed into the person God can use for good.

When Peter preached in the temple, he told his audience to "Repent therefore, and turn back, that your sins may be blotted out, that times of refreshing may come from the presence of the Lord, and that he may send the Christ appointed for you, Jesus" (Acts 3:19). The refreshing Peter spoke of comes from the Holy Spirit God places in us. With "Christ in me" I am being transformed into a new life. That transformation is a lifelong process of releasing the power. It is the process of hearing and pursuing his call in our lives. At salvation, Christ comes in to us to fill the void or vacuum in our lives. We gain a life of hope, peace, and power by which we can advance his kingdom. By making Jesus Lord, the Spirit is released to do the work and will of the Father.

From the perspective of the Old Testament, God's intention was that the Israelites proceed from the Red Sea to Kadesh Barnea and then into the promised land, a land filled with milk and honey. While the Red Sea represents **salvation,** the promised land represents **sanctification** or spiritual transformation, the process of God moving us from who we are to who he wants us to be. It is the process of setting aside the old life for the new life he offers. It is the process of eliminating those things that interfere with our relationship with him.

Israel's journey from the Red Sea to Kadesh Barnea took two-and-one-half years, not because it was a great distance (about 200 miles on a direct route) but because there were things the Lord wanted to teach his people. He led them south along the Red Sea to Mount Sinai and then north to Kadesh Barnea, nearly 600 miles. During this journey, the Lord discipled them, preparing them for life in the promised land. That process included developing obedience, persistence, boldness, and, most importantly, faith and dependence on God. For us, spiritual transformation is a similar process. It involves experiencing the power of God in overcoming obstacles to spiritual growth, being equipped for service, and living an empowered life.

Have you turned your life over to the Lord? Are you growing in the Lord?

Christ in me: becoming Christlike.

THE ABUNDANT LIFE

"The thief comes only to steal and kill and destroy. I came that they may have life and have it abundantly" (John 10:10).

> With salvation, the Lord offers us an abundant or Spirit-filled life. Just as he promised Israel land filled with milk and honey, he promises us the abundant life.

The Promised Land

The Lord made a covenant with Abram that his offspring would possess the promised land:

> "To your offspring I give this land, from the river of Egypt to the great river, the river Euphrates, the land of the Kenites, the Kenizzites, the Kadmonites, the Hittites, the Perizzites, the Rephaim, the Amorites, the Canaanites, the Girgashites and the Jebusites" (Gen. 15:18–21).

34

"I have come down to deliver them out of the hand of the Egyptians and to bring them up out of that land **to a good and broad land, a land flowing with milk and honey,** to the place of the Canaanites, the Hittites, the Amorites, the Perizzites, the Hivites, and the Jebusites" (Exod. 3:8, emphasis added).

There are fifteen references to a land flowing with milk and honey in Exodus, Leviticus, Numbers, and Deuteronomy. While the journey was difficult for the children of Israel, God held that promise in front of them. He continued to remind Israel that he had a place for them.

The Abundant Life

The abundant life comes with "Christ in me." This is what Paul describes in Romans:

You, however, are not in the flesh but in the Spirit, **if in fact the Spirit of God dwells in you.** Anyone who does not have the Spirit of Christ does not belong to him. But if Christ is in you, although the body is dead because of sin, the Spirit is life because of righteousness. If the Spirit of him who raised Jesus from the dead dwells in you, **he who raised Christ Jesus from the dead will also give life to your mortal bodies through his Spirit who dwells in you** (Rom. 8:9–11, emphasis added).

Paul said that those who have been saved are not of the flesh. He said that we can be victors in overcoming the struggles, temptations, and distractions of life.

"To them God chose to make known how great among the Gentiles are the riches of the glory of this mystery, **which is Christ in you,** the hope of glory" (Col. 1:27, emphasis added).

Paul informed the Colossians that they could unlock the mysteries of God—his plan for the world and his plan for individuals. The revelation of that plan comes through the indwelling Christ. Once we are assured of our salvation, understand "Christ in me," and release the power of the Spirit, we are given the desire to go deeper with Christ. Unleashing the Spirit is an intentional decision to surrender to the Lord, submit to him, and turn control of our lives over to him. This act of release is a deliberate decision to live a life led by the Spirit. Furthermore, it is a process. It is surrendering to him as much as we understand about him. As we mature spiritually, it becomes a daily surrender and then a moment-by-moment surrender.

Peter is an example of "Christ in me" when he preached to the Jews at Pentecost. He was an uneducated fisherman. The sermons he preached in Acts 2 and 3 were from the Holy Spirit. What he wrote in his two epistles was from the Holy Spirit—and he knew it:

> If anyone speaks, *let him speak* as the oracles of God. If anyone ministers, *let him do it* as **with the ability which God supplies**, that in all things God may be glorified through Jesus Christ, to whom belong the glory and the dominion forever and ever. Amen" (1 Pet. 4:11, NKJV, emphasis added).

As disciples, we need to encourage people to engage in activities that build a firm foundation of faith. We often depend on pulpit ministry, Sunday school, and fellowship to move people along on their spiritual journey. These are important. However, more personal discipling, such as small groups or mentoring, advances people on their spiritual journey more effectively and gives them a foundation on which pulpit ministry, Sunday school, and fellowship become more meaningful. Once the children of Israel crossed the Red Sea, God prepared them for entering the promised land. He did not leave them on their own. He discipled them.

Are you experiencing the abundant life?

Christ in me: the abundant life.

THE JOURNEY TO KADESH BARNEA

> I appeal to you therefore, brothers, by the mercies of
> God, to present your bodies as a living sacrifice, holy
> and acceptable to God, which is your spiritual worship.
> Do not be conformed to this world, but be transformed
> by the renewal of your mind, that by testing you may
> discern what is the will of God, what is good and
> acceptable and perfect (Rom. 12:1–2).

We are promised a new life at salvation. But that new life is a challenge. We are stuck in the old ways of thinking, old habits, and old desires. We remain conformed to the world. Ligon Duncan, scholar and pastor, has said, "There is a god we want and a God who is and the two are not the same." Spiritual transformation is the lifelong process of engaging the God who is and becoming productive members of his family.

God's desire is for us to move beyond salvation to discipleship. Discipleship means developing a personal relationship with the Lord and having a growing reliance on him that will carry us through life. Discipleship is a process of being spiritually transformed. It is the ever-increasing experience of the abundant life—living life to its fullest. God took specific actions to provide Israel a solid foundation of faith to prepare them for entering the promised land. We get a clear picture of that process in the books of Exodus, Leviticus, and Numbers. He began that process while Israel was still in Egypt and continued it during their journey to the promised land. Figure 1 is the commonly accepted map of the Israelites' journey from Egypt to the promised land.

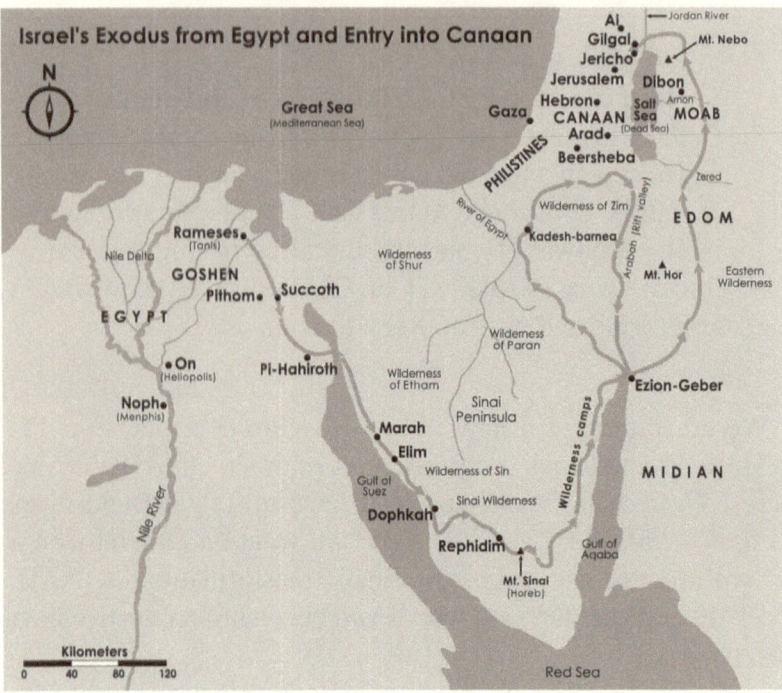

Figure 1. Exodus of Israel from Egypt into the Promised Land

Lord, Set Them Apart

> "There shall be one law for the native and for the stranger who sojourns among you" (Exod. 12:49).

Before leading Israel across the Red Sea, God demonstrated his power over life and death with the Passover. The Lord set Israel apart as he punished the Egyptians for failing to release his people (Exod. 12-13). *As believers, we need to understand that by personally accepting the blood shed by Christ, he forgives our sin and moves us from death into both a present and eternal fellowship with him which Paul described in this way:*

> "I am sending you to open their eyes, so that they may turn from darkness to light and from the power of

Satan to God, that they may receive forgiveness of sins and **a place among those who are sanctified by faith in me**" (Acts 26:17b–18 NLT, emphasis added).

The Lord Gave Them Direction

"And the Lord went before them by day in a pillar of cloud to lead them along the way, and by night in a pillar of fire to give them light, that they might travel by day and by night. The pillar of cloud by day and the pillar of fire by night did not depart from before the people" (Exod. 13:21–22).

God gave them direction with the pillars of cloud by day and fire by night as he led them in the desert to the Red Sea (Exod. 13). He continued to lead them in that manner from the Red Sea to Kadesh Barnea and from Kadesh Barnea to the promised land. He guided them. God was with them. *He has told us that he will lead us during the day (times of joy and celebration) and during the night (times of despair and helplessness). Jesus promised his disciples that he would lead them in service and ministry.*

"And he said to them, 'Follow me, and I will make you fishers of men.' Immediately they left their nets and followed him" (Matt. 4:19–20).

The Lord Delivered Them from Death

Then Moses stretched out his hand over the sea, and the Lord drove the sea back by a strong east wind all night and made the sea dry land, and the waters were divided. And the people of Israel went into the midst of the sea on dry ground, the waters being a wall to them on their right hand and on their left (Exod. 14:21–22).

God led Israel to the banks of the Red Sea. At that point, Israel had two options: return to slavery in Egypt or trust the Lord for deliverance. He then delivered them from the Egyptians (Exodus 14). *The Lord leads us to a point where we need to choose between staying where we are or moving to freedom in him. He gives us the freedom to choose eternal life or eternal death.*

> "And as Moses lifted up the serpent in the wilderness, so must the Son of Man be lifted up, that whoever believes in him may have eternal life" (John 3:14–15).

The Lord Gave Them Joy

> "And he cried to the Lord, and the Lord showed him a log, and he threw it into the water, and the water became sweet" (Exod. 15:25).

Three days after crossing the Red Sea, they were in the desert of Shur and encountered bitter water. The people grumbled. The Lord turned the bitter water at Marah into sweet water. The Lord then challenged them to listen to him, be obedient, and that he would keep them from the diseases he inflicted on the Egyptians (Exod. 16:2–3). *For us, he changes the bitterness of life into the sweetness of the Holy Spirit; Christ in me. He blesses our obedience.*

> "These things I have spoken to you, that my joy may be in you, and that your joy may be full" (John 15:11).

The Lord Fed Them

> "In the evening quail came up and covered the camp, and in the morning...there was on the face of the wilderness a fine, flake-like thing, fine as frost on the ground" (Exod. 16:13-15).

The people grumbled for the second time because they had run out of food. God provided quail and manna for them daily from that time until they entered the promised land. *The lesson for us is that*

God provides spiritual food for our souls. He provides the Word for our spiritual growth and daily life.

"I am the living bread that came down from heaven. If anyone eats of this bread, he will live forever. And the bread that I will give for the life of the world is my flesh" (John 6:51).

The Lord Provided Water

> "'Behold, I will stand before you there on the rock at Horeb, and you shall strike the rock, and water shall come out of it, and the people will drink.' And Moses did so, in the sight of the elders of Israel" (Exod. 17:6).

Upon moving from the Wilderness of Sin, the people grumbled for the third time because they were again without water. The Lord instructed Moses to strike the rock with his staff, and water poured out of the rock. Water is essential for life. Again, the Lord met their needs. *We need to know that he meets our needs too.*

> "Jesus answered her, 'If you knew the gift of God, and who it is that is saying to you, 'Give me a drink,' you would have asked him, and he would have given you living water'" (John 4:10).

The Lord Brought Victory

> "But Moses' hands grew weary, so they took a stone and put it under him, and he sat on it, while Aaron and Hur held up his hands, one on one side, and the other on the other side. So his hands were steady until the going down of the sun. And Joshua overwhelmed Amalek and his people with the sword" (Exod. 17:12–13).

When the Amalekites attacked Israel at Rephidim, the Lord gave them victory. Recall that Israel advanced when Aaron and Hur held up Moses's arms and retreated when they let Moses's arms down. The Lord fought for Israel. He was a proven victor in battle if the people moved out in faith. The Lord was preparing Israel for the battles they would face in removing the occupants of the promised land. *We need to know that the Lord is with us in our battles against the enemy and in overcoming the trials and tribulations we face in our spiritual journey.*

> "For everyone who has been born of God overcomes the world. And this is the victory that has overcome the world—our faith. Who is it that overcomes the world except the one who believes that Jesus is the Son of God?" (1 John 5:4–5).

The Lord Established a Covenant with Them

> "'You yourselves have seen what I did to the Egyptians, and how I bore you on eagles' wings and brought you to myself. Now therefore, if you will indeed obey my voice and keep my covenant, you shall be my treasured possession among all peoples, for all the earth is mine; and you shall be to me a kingdom of priests and a holy nation.' These are the words that you shall speak to the people of Israel." And God spoke all these words, saying, "I am the Lord your God, who brought you out of the land of Egypt, out of the house of slavery" (Exod. 19:5–6).

God's covenant was with Israel and no one else. He called them to be a holy nation. The Israelites' identity was to be in him. He set them apart for his purposes among all the people of the earth. He made it clear to the Israelites through the plagues upon Egypt that they were different from the Egyptians because they were not affected by the plagues. With the tenth plague, the Israelites needed covering or protection from the "angel of death." They set themselves apart by placing the blood of an unblemished lamb on the doorposts and lintels of their homes. Moreover, the children of Israel knew their genealogical roots. They were descendants of Jacob. Under God's direction, they settled in Goshen and remained separate in customs, beliefs, and location from the Egyptians. When he established his covenant with them, he became their God and not just the God of their forefathers.

God established a new covenant with us under the blood shed by his Son. He gives us an identity as his children. We are his, set apart among all the peoples of the earth. We must establish our own relationship with him. Faith is no longer a matter of believing in the God of our parents. Faith is a matter of having a personal relationship with him.

> "Such is the confidence that we have through Christ toward God. Not that we are sufficient in ourselves to claim anything as coming from us, but our sufficiency is from God, who has made us sufficient to be ministers of a new covenant, not of the letter but of the Spirit. For the letter kills, but the Spirit gives life" (2 Cor. 3:4–6).

The Lord Set Boundaries for Living

> "And God spoke all these words, saying, 'I am the Lord your God, who brought you out of the land of Egypt, out of the house of slavery. You shall have no other gods before me'" (Exod. 20:1–3).

He gave Israel the Ten Commandments and laws to live by (Exod. 20-24). *He gave us his Word to tell us how to live.*

> "All Scripture is breathed out by God and profitable for teaching, for reproof, for correction, and for training in righteousness, that the man of God may be complete, equipped for every good work" (2 Tim. 3:16–17).

The Lord Gave Them a Pattern of Worship

> "And let them make me a sanctuary, that I may dwell in their midst. Exactly as I show you concerning the pattern of the tabernacle, and of all its furniture, so you shall make it" (Exod. 25:8–9).

He gave them instructions on how to worship him, when to worship, how to sacrifice, and how to consecrate the priests (Exod. 25–31). He set his people apart from the pagan cultures they would face in the promised land. *This tells us that worship is to be an important and routine part of our lives.*

> "Our fathers worshiped on this mountain, but you say that in Jerusalem is the place where people ought to worship." Jesus said to her, "Woman, believe me, the hour is coming when neither on this mountain nor in Jerusalem will you worship the Father. You worship what you do not know; we worship what we know, for salvation is from the Jews. But the hour is coming, and is now here, when the true worshipers will worship the Father in spirit and truth, for the Father is seeking such people to worship him" (John 4:20–23).

The Lord Established Holy Ground

> "Now Moses used to take the tent and pitch it outside the camp, far off from the camp, and he called it the tent of meeting. And everyone who sought the Lord would go out to the tent of meeting, which was outside the camp" (Exod. 33:7).

He provided a place where the people could go to meet God away from the turmoil of the camp (the tent of meeting*). He expects us to carve out a time and place in our busy, cluttered lives to have quality time with him.*

> "But when you pray, go into your room and shut the door and pray to your Father who is in secret. And

your Father who sees in secret will reward you" (Matt. 6: 6).

"And he said to them, "Come away by yourselves to a desolate place and rest a while." For many were coming and going, and they had no leisure even to eat" (Mark 6:31).

The Lord Gave Them Spiritual Direction

"The Lord called Moses and spoke to him from the tent of meeting, saying, "Speak to the people of Israel and say to them, When any one of you brings an offering to the Lord, you shall bring your offering of livestock from the herd or from the flock" (Lev. 1:1–2).

He gave them directions for living a life set apart from the people around them and called for obedience and holiness (the book of Leviticus). *Consider Jesus and the apostles' words to us:*

"And when they bring you before the synagogues and the rulers and the authorities, do not be anxious about how you should defend yourself or what you should say, for the Holy Spirit will teach you in that very hour what you ought to say" (Luke 12:11–12).

"I write these things to you about those who are trying to deceive you. But the anointing that you received from him abides in you, and you have no need that anyone should teach you. But as his anointing teaches you about everything, and is true, and is no lie—just as it has taught you, abide in him" (1 John 2:26–27).

The Lord Prepared His People

During their time in the desert, the Lord prepared Israel to meet the challenges they would face upon entering the promised land. His preparation was complete when they arrived at Kadesh-Barnea. The people were ready to enter the promised land. *He gives us what we need to carry out the tasks he gives us and the challenges we will face.*

1. Have you made the transition of faith from your parents' God to a personal faith?
2. Have you surrendered your life to him?
3. Have you put him in charge of your life?
4. Are you aware of God's presence in your life?
5. What has he been saying to you?
6. What direction is he giving you?
7. Is he meeting your spiritual needs?

God's plan in discipling believers is to prepare them to be productive, experience the ever-increasing blessings of abundant life, and gain the confidence needed to meet life's challenges. Through the mentoring of "Christ in me," we undergo spiritual transformation. This includes the process of:

- Making God's plans our needs
- Setting aside the old life for the new life
- Gaining a biblical view of the purpose for our lives
- Building a faith to carry us through trials and tribulation Are you being discipled?

Christ in me: making me new.

THE REBELLION AT KADESH BARNEA

"Not one shall come into the land where I swore that I would make you dwell, except Caleb the son of Jephunneh and Joshua the son of Nun. But your little ones, who you said would become a prey, I will bring in, and they shall know the land that you have rejected" (Num. 14:30).

After two-and-a-half years in the desert, God completed preparing the Israelites to enter the promised land. Moses sent twelve spies into Canaan. After forty days, the spies returned and reported to the people. Joshua and Caleb provided a glowing report indicating that the land was theirs for the taking. The other ten spies reported that the situation was impossible. The land was filled with giants.

The Lord, by a powerful display of his authority over nature and man, delivered Israel from Pharaoh and the Amalekites and provided them food, water, and direction. Despite that awesome display of power, the Israelites saw the promised land as an impossibility. The children of Israel did not believe that God would or could overcome the obstacles reported by the ten spies. They rejected the report of Joshua and Caleb and refused to move forward (Num. 13–14).

They saw the challenge through human eyes. The risk was too great; the obstacles were impossible. "We cannot succeed in conquering the land!" They did not have faith that God would bring victory (as he had in the past). As a result, God sentenced them to wander in the desert for the next forty years. Those were forty years of anguish and frustration. The people were without rest. The promised land was just that: a promise, not a reality. Once the faithless generation passed away, the people were ready to move forward. Only when unbelief died could Israel enter and subdue the promised land. The people of Israel grumbled when things did not go their way.
They seemed to always be on the verge of rebellion against Moses and Aaron, and through them, against God.

Then there was a perceived need: a connection with God. When Moses had been on Mount Sinai for forty days, the Israelites thought he had died and that their connection to the Lord was gone and they created the golden calf (Exod. 32).

After forty years and the death of the rebelling generation, the people moved forward in faith without hesitation. Israel marched north through Edom, Moab, Ammon, and Bashan. Under the Lord's command, they defeated the armies of Sihon and Og. Israel moved purposefully into the promised land under the Lord's direction and under Joshua's leadership. They believed the Lord would meet their needs and fight their battles. There was no debate. The promised land became a reality.

Like Israel, moving into the abundant life requires a decision, a commitment to place our lives under the authority of the Lord. The decision is to stay where we are or turning our lives over to the power that lives in us. Are we ready to leave the old life behind? Do we really believe that the Lord can change our lives? Can the Lord really overcome the giants in our lives?

The writer of Hebrews warns about ignoring God's call to surrender, of neglecting to bring our lives under his control.

> Therefore, as the Holy Spirit says "Today, if you hear his voice, do not harden your hearts as in the rebellion, on the day of testing in the wilderness, where your fathers put me to the test and saw my works for forty years. Therefore I was provoked with that generation, and said, 'They always go astray in their heart; they have not known my ways.' As I swore in my wrath, 'They shall not enter my rest'" (Heb. 3:7–10).

Are you advancing under God's direction, or are you rebelling?

Christ in me: faith and courage to move forward.

THE VINE AND BRANCHES

> "I am the vine; you are the branches. Whoever abides in me and I in him, he it is that bears much fruit, for apart from me you can do nothing" (John 15:5).

The night before he was betrayed, Jesus explained his expectations for his disciples with the allegory of the vine and branches in the upper room. He was preparing his disciples for life without his physical presence. He pointed out three essential relationships: their relationship with the Father, their relationship with each other, and their relationship with the world. Through this allegory, he challenged his disciples to be productive.

Pruning

> "I am the true vine, and my Father is the vinedresser. Every branch in me that does not bear fruit he takes away, and every branch that does bear fruit he prunes, that it may bear more fruit" (John 15:1–2).

It is through the Father's effort as the vinedresser that the vine produces the desired quantity and quality of fruit. First, the vinedresser takes away branches that do not bear fruit. The unfruitful branches, which may be dead or diseased, are removed so that nutrients flow to the healthy branches. The second step is pruning healthy branches so they can bear more fruit. Jesus made a clear distinction between cutting off and pruning. Cutting off is the final judgment and pruning is for increased productivity.

Abide in Me[26]

> "Already you are clean because of the word that I have spoken to you. Abide in me, and I in you. As the branch cannot bear fruit by itself, unless it abides in the vine, neither can you, unless you abide in me" (John 15:34).

Jesus told His disciples: "You are cleansed and pruned already, because of the word I have given you (the teachings I have discussed with you)" (John 15:3 AMP). The disciples were prepared by the vinedresser to produce fruit through his words. The writer of Hebrews states, "For the word of God is living and active, sharper than any two-edged sword, piercing to the division of soul and of spirit, of joints and of marrow, and discerning the thoughts and intentions of the heart" (Heb. 4:12).

Jesus stated that the quality of the connection between the vine and branches is essential to produce good fruit. As believers, we are to abide in him and he in us. By being in him, we are protected from the wrath of God. By him being in us, we are empowered by the Holy Spirit to produce fruit.

Remain in Me

> I am the vine; you are the branches. Whoever abides in
> me and I in him, he it is that bears much fruit, for
> apart from me you can do nothing. If anyone does not
> abide in me he is thrown away like a branch and
> withers; and the branches are gathered, thrown into
> the fire, and burned. If you abide in me, and my words
> abide in you, ask whatever you wish, and it will be done
> for you. By this my Father is glorified, that you bear
> much fruit and so prove to be my disciples (John 15:5–
> 8).

Jesus expanded the metaphor with three promises. First, by
remaining in him, we will bear much fruit. Our connection to Jesus
must be solid. Only then will we receive the spiritual nourishment to be
Christ to the world. "Apart from me you can do nothing" means we
cannot be of eternal value in the kingdom unless we are steadfastly
connected to Jesus. When we are connected to Jesus, "Christ in me"
will flow out. Second, those not abiding in him will be cast off as
useless and destroyed by fire. There is a sense of immediacy, finality,
and judgment in these words. Third, by Jesus remaining in us and we
in him, he will grant all we ask. Jesus granting our requests only comes
under two conditions: we are in him (salvation), and he is in us
(sanctification). Jesus said that by being solidly connected to him, what
we ask will be in his will. He concludes that by "remaining in him," we
will bear much fruit. Bearing much fruit is the mark of a disciple.

Love and Joy

> "As the Father has loved me, so have I loved you.
> Abide in my love. If you keep my commandments, you
> will abide in my love, just as I have kept my Father's
> commandments and abide in his love. These things I
> have spoken to you, that my joy may be in you, and that
> your joy may be full" (John 15:9–11).

Jesus said that love unites disciples with the Lord and with others. Next, he links his love to our obedience, that is, keeping his commands. He then states that joy flows from him into the disciples so that their joy will flow out into the world. Obedience comes from Jesus in us. Jesus in us brings joy.

Love One Another

> "This is my commandment, that you love one another as I have loved you. Greater love has no one than this, that someone lay down his life for his friends" (John 15:12–13).

Only through love can we, as disciples, move forward in unity. Advancing the kingdom is not about us. We are only able to bear fruit through the power of the Spirit within us. Bearing fruit requires setting aside our personal desires and will for that of the Lord. We must lay our lives aside so the Lord can have his way. Laying down our lives requires sacrifice, giving up our rights, time, talents, and treasure for his kingdom. This is not a suggestion; it is a command. The relationship between disciples is measured by His love.

Friends

> "You are my friends if you do what I command you. No longer do I call you servants, for the servant does not know what his master is doing; but I have called you friends, for all that I have heard from my Father I have made known to you" (John 15:14–15).

Jesus addressed the disciples as friends by comparing their relationship to the relationship between servants and masters. By being connected to the vine, we know the Lord's will and his plans. He has and continues to impart his plans and will to us through the presence of the Spirit. As his friends and confidents, we know his plans and make them our own.

By Jesus's definition, disciples are partners. They are empowered to carry out God's plan. As his partners, we adopt his plans as our own. By doing so, we are assured that we are engaged in carrying out his plan and know that God will bring it to a successful conclusion.

Appointed to Bear Fruit

> "You did not choose me, but I chose you and appointed you that you should go and bear fruit and that your fruit should abide, so that whatever you ask the Father in my name, he may give it to you. These things I command you, so that you will love one another" (John 15:16–17).

Jesus chose his disciples to bear lasting fruit. He repeated his promise that he would give them whatever they asked if they were obedient. By being solidly connected to the vine, the power of the Spirit flows through us, producing much fruit according to the plan that God reveals to us.

Jesus taught the disciples that they would:

- Be pruned to be more productive
- Understand his will and plans
- Keep his commands resulting in love, joy, and unity among the disciples
- Be his partners in advancing his kingdom
- Bear much fruit

Have you experienced "Christ in me?"

Christ in me: producing fruit.

WALKING BY THE SPIRIT

"But I say, walk by the Spirit, and you will not gratify the desires of the flesh. For the desires of the flesh are against the Spirit, and the desires of the Spirit are against the flesh, for these are opposed to each other, to keep you from doing the things you want to do. But if you are led by the Spirit, you are not under the law" (Gal. 5:16–18).

The pruning in the preceding allegory translates into removing our hidden faults, presumptive sin, and bondage and addiction.

Hidden Faults

The psalmist said, "Who can discern his errors? Declare me innocent from hidden faults" (Ps. 19:12). Hidden faults take two forms. First, they are sins of which we are not aware. They are behaviors that may be a routine part of our life and our interactions with others but do not glorify God. In fact, they may undermine our testimony. Second, hidden faults are thoughts or attitudes to which we rent space in our heads. They can be vain imaginations that no one knows about. The problem is that they can take on an outward expression in inappropriate words or actions. The psalmist's cry was to be rescued from hidden faults.

Solution: Recognize the fault by the prompting of the Spirit or through accountability. Then confess the fault, repent, and surrender to the power of the Spirit within to set things right.

Presumptive Sin

> "Keep back your servant also from presumptuous sins;
> Let them not have dominion over me. Then I shall be
> blameless, and innocent of great transgression. Let the
> words of my mouth and the meditation of my heart be
> acceptable in your sight, O Lord, my rock and my
> redeemer" (Ps. 19:13–14).

Presumptive sin gets its name from a person's presumption or belief that their sins have been covered at the cross. They know what they are doing is wrong but do it anyway. The concern here is the unavoidable barrier sin creates between us and the Lord. Any sin is a barrier. We mistakenly believe all that is needed is self-discipline. Self-discipline deals with the surface issue and not its root. We need to drill down and ask what motivates the thought or action. Is it selfish desire, self-importance, or an idol? Who is at the center of your life? The psalmist's cry was that presumptive sin did not have control over him.

Solution: Like hidden faults, presumptive sin can only be removed by the Holy Spirit. We must recognize the fault, confess, repent, and surrender to the power of the Spirit within to set things right.

Bondage and Addiction

When the Israelites crossed the Jordan River, they encountered Jericho, a major fortified city that was shut up and had to be removed before they could move on. However, the city was not destroyed by siege or the army of Israel, but by the Lord.

There are inappropriate attitudes and behaviors that we just cannot shake. While we may be under conviction that we need to eliminate them, nothing seems to work. No matter how hard we try, they just will not go away. We discover that self-discipline is a patch on old cloth and therefore fails. Obedience eludes us.

Like Jericho, addictions appear impossible to overcome. They are giants in the land. They loom over our lives like Tyrannosaurus Rex and will not go away. We recognize that there is nothing we can do about it. We are powerless, helpless. The bondage is shut up tight. And just saying "No" does not work. The bondage controls us. Yet, Christ in me, the Holy Spirit, the power within us overcomes bondage.

"For everyone who has been born of God overcomes the world. And this is the victory that has overcome the world—our faith. Who is it that overcomes the world except the one who believes that Jesus is the Son of God?" (1 John 5:4–5).

Likewise the Spirit helps us in our weakness. For we do not know what to pray for as we ought, but the Spirit himself intercedes for us with groanings too deep for words. And he who searches hearts knows what is the mind of the Spirit, because the Spirit intercedes for the saints according to the will of God. And we know that for those who love God all things work together for good, for those who are called according to his purpose (Rom. 8:26–28).

"No, in all these things we are more than conquerors through him who loved us. For I am sure that neither death nor life, nor angels nor rulers, nor things present nor things to come, nor powers, nor height nor depth, nor anything else in all creation, will be able to separate us from the love of God in Christ Jesus our Lord" (Rom. 8:37–39).

"In him you also, when you heard the word of truth, the gospel of your salvation, and believed in him, were sealed with the promised Holy Spirit, who is the guarantee of our inheritance until we acquire possession of it, to the praise of his glory" (Eph. 1:13–14).

In Summary

The following tools are available for unleashing the power within us in dealing with hidden faults, presumptive sin, and bondage.

- Confession
- Repentance
- Believe – having faith that "Christ in me" will overcome
- Absolute surrender – admission that we are powerless in dealing with sin
- Prayer and fasting
- Praying back verses on victory

George Pardington states that to overcome sin and bondage, we must believe that the Lord will bring victory.

> How, then, may the vision of victory be transformed into the realization of victory? By the definite reception of the gift of the Holy Ghost through a step of entire surrender and an act of appropriating faith. We have already seen that the holiness of the Christian flows from contact with God. This contact has both a Divine and a human side. On the Divine side there are two points of contact, namely: the identification of the believer with Christ in His death and resurrection and the definite reception of the gift of the Holy Ghost. On the human side there are also two points of contact, namely: a step of entire surrender and the receiving of the Holy Ghost through an act of appropriating faith.[27]

This concept that "Christ in me" overcomes sin rocks my boat. I am not satisfied with my walk. I struggle with inappropriate attitudes and behavior. On the other hand, I can look back on my life and see changes that are not the result of self-discipline or my own efforts. I am being transformed. Transformation is the result of his power working in my life.

Christian psychologist, Larry Crabb, takes the following approach in helping people understand their sin. He asks them to consider their feelings, the behavior that led to those feelings, the choice that led to the behavior, and the core values that led to the choice.[28] Crabb's bottom line is this: When dealing with sin, we need to define what is at the center of our lives. Is it our perceived needs? Is it power, possessions, or prestige? Who is in charge, me, or the Lord? Have you tried to fix the problem? How are your efforts working for you? Who is at the center of your life?

Christ in me: the power to overcome.

TRIALS AND TRIBULATION

Understanding Trials and Tribulation

> "No test or temptation that comes your way is beyond the course of what others have had to face. All you need to remember is that God will never let you down; he'll never let you be pushed past your limit; he'll always be there to help you come through it" (1 Cor. 10:13 MSG).

After World War II, British automaker, Rolls Royce, discovered that its clientele had changed. Instead of buying the luxury car to be chauffeur-driven, the buyers were driving the cars themselves. So, Rolls Royce began installing Borg Warner automatic transmissions. Shortly thereafter, the transmissions began to fail. Borg Warner was called in to investigate the problem. When the inspectors opened the failed transmissions, they discovered that Rolls Royce had polished all the internal workings. When asked why, Rolls Royce explained that they would not sell cars with imperfections. Borg Warner explained that the rough areas were needed to move fluid throughout the transmission to keep it lubricated.

Rough spots are important for spiritual growth and building faith.

They lubricate our faith. It is difficult to understand this while going through troubled times. When experiencing trials, we might ask, "Why me?" Instead, we need to ask, "What are you saying to me, Lord?" or "How can you use this difficulty to advance your kingdom?" Usually, the answer to these questions does not come until we have gone through the difficulty and can look back.

We know from Satan's conversation with God about Job that the difficulties we face in life do not come from God but Satan. Satan is active and works to get us offtrack. He wants us to deny our faith or curse God. In the above verse, Paul makes it clear that God does not allow more pain and suffering than we can bear. In Job's case, God said, "Thus far shall you come, and no farther, and here shall your proud waves be stayed" (Job 38:22). If this is the case for creation, then his promise for us is that he will not allow our trials to exceed what we can endure. The Bible has many verses about facing trials and suffering. The main people who are quoted in these verses (Jesus Christ, Job, and disciples Paul, Peter, and James) went through some of the most intense suffering and trials any man has ever known. Here are some notable verses that demonstrate why God allows us to go through the fire of turmoil and suffering:

Table 1. Why God Allows Pain and Suffering

Scriptures about Suffering	The Purpose of Suffering Is to:
"[God] comforts us in all our troubles, so that we can comfort those in any trouble with the comfort we ourselves have received from God" (2 Cor. 1:4).	Equip us to comfort others in similar situations
"And we know that in all things God works for the good of those who love him, who have been called according to his purpose" (Rom. 8:28).	Achieve his purpose even though that may be unknown at the time

"I know that you can do all things, and that no purpose of yours can be thwarted. 'Who is this that hides counsel without knowledge?' Therefore I have uttered what I did not understand, things too wonderful for me, which I did not know" (Job 42:2–3).	Bring about a deeper knowledge and understanding of God and his sovereignty
"Dear friends, do not be surprised at the painful trial you are suffering, as though something strange were happening to you. But rejoice that you participate in the sufferings of Christ, so that you may be overjoyed when his glory is revealed" (1 Pet. 4:12–13).	Bring us the joy of knowing that we join Christ in his suffering
For this light momentary affliction is preparing for us an eternal weight of glory beyond all comparison, as we look not to the things that are seen but to the things that are unseen. For the things that are seen are transient, but the things that are unseen are eternal. (2 Cor. 4:17–18).	Move our focus away from the temporal to the permanent (eternal)
"Consider it pure joy, my brothers, whenever you face trials of many kinds, because you know that the testing of your faith develops perseverance. Perseverance must finish its work so that you may be mature and complete, not lacking anything" (James 1:2–4).	Develop perseverance, which leads to spiritual maturity

Brothers, as an example of patience in the face of suffering, take the prophets who spoke in the name of the Lord. As you know, we consider blessed those who have persevered. You have heard of Job's perseverance and have seen what the Lord finally brought about. The Lord is full of compassion and mercy (James 5:10–11).	Experience the Lord's mercy and compassion
Not only so, but we also rejoice in our sufferings, because we know that suffering produces perseverance; perseverance, character; and character, hope. And hope does not disappoint us, because God has poured out his love into our hearts by the Holy Spirit, whom he has given us (Rom. 5:3–5).	Grow in perseverance, which builds character that leads to hope
"I consider that our present sufferings are not worth comparing with the glory that will be revealed in us" (Rom. 8:18).	Remind us that we live in a fallen world and that we are destined for the joy of the eternal presence of the Lord
But this happened that we might not rely on ourselves but on God, who raises the dead. He has delivered us from such a deadly peril, and he will deliver us. On him we have set our hope that he will continue to deliver us, as you help us by your prayers. Then many will give thanks on our behalf for the gracious favor granted us in answer to the prayers of many (2 Cor. 1:9–11).	Teach us dependence on the Lord and give others the opportunity to minister in prayer and see God at work

"Although he was a son, [Jesus] learned obedience through what he suffered" (Heb. 5:8).	Learn obedience
In this you rejoice, though now for a little while, if necessary, you have been grieved by various trials, so that the tested genuineness of your faith— more precious than gold that perishes though it is tested by fire— may be found to result in praise and glory and honor at the revelation of Jesus Christ (1 Pet. 1:6–7).	Refine our faith and bring glory and honor to Jesus
"So to keep me from becoming conceited because of the surpassing greatness of the revelations, a thorn was given me in the flesh, a messenger of Satan to harass me, to keep me from becoming conceited" (2 Cor. 12:7).	Teach us humility
"For the sake of Christ, then, I am content with weaknesses, insults, hardships, persecutions, and calamities. For when I am weak, then I am strong" (2 Cor. 12:10).	Develop our dependence on the Lord and strength in weakness
"Every branch in me that does not bear fruit he takes away, and every branch that does bear fruit he prunes, that it may bear more fruit" (John 15:2).	Improve productivity

We also need to remember that we go through sufferings because we are on the front line of advancing his kingdom. We are in the war between the Lord and Satan. Satan's intent is to destroy the kingdom of God. But be encouraged, we are not in the battle alone.

> "For we do not wrestle against flesh and blood, but against the rulers, against the authorities, against the cosmic powers over this present darkness, against the spiritual forces of evil in the heavenly places" (Eph. 6:12).

> "And that all this assembly may know that the Lord saves not with sword and spear. For the battle is the Lord's, and he will give you into our hand" (1 Sam. 17:24).

> "The good news is that after the suffering "the God of all grace, who has called you to his eternal glory in Christ, will himself restore, confirm, strengthen, and establish you" (1 Pet. 5:10).

During trials and tribulations, it is always good to remember, as Bible teacher Warren Wiersby wrote: "When God puts His children in the furnace of adversity, His loving hand knows how long and how much. He keeps His eye on the thermostat, and His hand on the dial."[29] Do you see the trials and tribulations of life as tools for growing in your faith?

Christ in me: the power to overcome.

THE PEACE OF GOD

> "But the Helper, the Holy Spirit, whom the Father will send in my name, he will teach you all things and bring to your remembrance all that I have said to you. **Peace I**

leave with you; my peace I give to you. Not as the world
gives do I give to you. Let not your hearts be troubled,
neither let them be afraid" (John 14:26–27, emphasis
added).

Recall that peace with God comes with salvation; the war is over.
The peace of God comes from "Christ in me." The peace of God
comes through surrender to the indwelling power of God.[30]
Paul expresses the peace of God as follows:

"And the peace of God, which surpasses all
understanding, will guard your hearts and your minds
in Christ Jesus" (Phil. 4:7, emphasis added).

"And let the peace of Christ rule in your hearts, to
which indeed you were called in one body. And be
thankful" (Col. 3:15, emphasis added).

Bible scholar Joseph Thayer defines the peace of God as the
tranquil state of a soul assured of its salvation through Christ, and so
fearing nothing from God and is content with its earthly lot, of
whatever sort that is.[31]
The peace of God is present despite turmoil and suffering. Peace is
to be lived out in a community of believers and in the world. The
peace of God sets the believer apart from the world. To live in peace is
to display "Christ in me" to the world.
Charles Spurgeon illustrated the peace of God with this story:

It is beautiful to see a child at perfect peace amid dangers
which alarm all those who are with him. I have read of a
little boy who was on board a vessel buffeted by the
storm, and everyone was afraid, knowing that the ship
was in grave danger. There was not a sailor on board,
certainly not a passenger, who was not alarmed. This boy,
however, was perfectly happy, and was rather amused
than frightened by the tossing of the ship. They asked
him why he was so happy at such a time. "Well," he said,

"my father is the captain. He knows how to manage."[32]

"You keep him in perfect peace whose mind is stayed on you, because he trusts in you" (Isa. 26:3).

Do you have the peace of God?

Christ in me: the peace that passes understanding.

LIVING ON INSTRUMENT FLIGHT RULES

On a Monday evening in mid-January 1980, three men from Texas took off in a single engine plane from the airfield at Breckenridge, Colorado, after a weekend of skiing. They headed east over the Front Range of the Rocky Mountains planning to land at Centennial Airport, southeast of Denver. The intent was to refuel before flying on to Texas. However, the airport was under heavy clouds. The field was not equipped for instrument landing, so FAA's Denver Center sent them to Buckley Air National Guard Base east of Denver because it was equipped with a radar approach control. The Buckley controller directed the pilot on a course aligned with the Buckley runway.

However, Buckley was also under heavy clouds, and the pilot could not see the airfield. He was not trained to fly under instrument flight rules (IFR). Under IFR, the pilot flies under the direction of a radar controller, with the instruments in front of him, and without external visual references. The Buckley controller began issuing instructions for the pilot to descend. The pilot refused to descend on the prescribed glide path because he could not see the ground.

The controller sent the plane around for a second attempt. The pilot made the loop and was again on the right course for landing. However, the moisture in the clouds froze on the wings of the plane until it could no longer fly. It crashed south of the field, killing all three men.

Think about the spiritual application in this accident: The radar controller knew exactly where the plane was and where it needed to be. God knows where we are and where we need to be and how to make that transition.

In the break room in the control tower that evening, the radar controller, who had directed the pilot, sat in the corner weeping uncontrollably. He had done everything he knew to get the pilot to descend. He did everything right. Are you aware that the God of Israel grieves at our unwillingness to allow him control of our lives?

> "Your eyes saw my unformed substance; in your book were written, every one of them, the days that were formed for me, when as yet there was none of them" (Ps. 139:16 NLT).

> "For I know the thoughts I think toward you, says the Lord, thoughts of peace and not of evil, to give you a future and a hope" (Jer. 29:11 NKJV).

It is God's intention that we enter the abundant life, the Spirit-filled life. God wants us to fly (live) by instrument flight rules (the Holy Spirit). Like a pilot, we need to be trained to trust God alone. God's plan is for us to live lives completely dependent on Him.

It is a matter of trust, yielding as much of ourselves to him as we understand of the power that is available to us in the person of the Holy Spirit.

Have you transferred control of your life to the one who knows where you are and where you need to be?

Christ in me: living life under the direction of the Holy Spirit.

THE DECISION

> "And it happened that while Apollos was at Corinth, Paul passed through the inland country and came to Ephesus. There he found some disciples. And he said to them, "Did you receive the Holy Spirit when you

believed?" And they said, "No, we have not even heard
that there is a Holy Spirit'" (Acts 19:1–3).

God intends for us to be a part of his kingdom. He invites us into
his family through salvation. God intends for us to enjoy the
abundant life. He placed his Spirit in us to clean up our lives and make us
productive members of his family. While we need to transfer trust from
ourselves to the Lord, we fear losing control. When the Lord leads in
a direction that takes us out of our comfort zone or asks us to do
something that is not in our tool kit, we make excuses, ignoring God's
direction. Like Israel, we grumble and rebel. Transferring trust means
moving from insisting on understanding things in a physical sense to
understanding things from a spiritual perspective. The Lord calls us
from virtual reality (the world as we see it) to the world as God sees it.

"Christ in me" helps us grow spiritually through prayer, worship, the
Word, and fellowship. He asks us to take on tasks that are impossible
for us. He wants to have control of our lives. Only then will he do
great and mighty things in and through us. If we do not transfer trust to
him, we are destined to wander in the desert until we experience the
death of unbelief. When we reach our personal Kadesh Barnea, we have
a choice, we can either transfer control of our lives to him, or we can
attempt to handle life on our own. We can rebel or surrender to the
power of Christ in me.

It is a matter of knowing that when the Lord asks us to do
something, he is the one who will do it (Christ in me). God said, "I can
and will lead you. Follow me!" It is God's hand in our glove.

God has a plan for us. He has promised us the abundant life, a land
of milk and honey. He will open the way for us if we turn over control
to him and accept the invitation to find the rest God has for us.[33] Our
choice is to move forward in faith or depend on our own strength and
wisdom. We may be overwhelmed by the perceived strongholds,
barriers, and giants we face. But we are overcomers because Christ is
in us. He is the overcomer. By his presence, we are empowered to
overcome.

Have you experienced the Overcomer in your life?

Christ in me: choosing to live an empowered life.

TRANSFERRING TRUST

Three words are frequently used to describe the act of transferring trust or control to the Lord: commitment, submission, and surrender. Below are the definitions of each illustrating the decisive action needed to unleash the power of the Holy Spirit.

Commitment. Biblical commitment is an intentional, voluntary decision to put the Lord in charge of our lives. It is the act of deciding to make Jesus the Lord of our lives. "Commit to the Lord whatever you do, and he will establish your plans" (Prov. 16:3 NIV). While commitment is a personal decision, the ability to keep that commitment is motivated by the Holy Spirit. To commit is to focus on the Lord.

Submission. Biblical submission is the personal and willing decision to place our lives under God's higher authority. Through faith in Christ, we receive his righteousness as our own and keep his commandments through the power of the Holy Spirit. Furthermore, Christ empowers us to follow him in submission.[34] Submission is a matter of giving him control of our lives. Submission is a daily decision that graduates into moment-by-moment decisions as we mature in the Lord. To submit is to be under the Lord's authority.

Surrender. Biblical surrender is the act of willfully relinquishing the control of our lives to the Lord. It involves two decisions. First, surrender is the conscious act of giving up living under our own wisdom and strength. Second, surrender is deliberately placing ourselves under the control of the Holy Spirit. "I have been crucified with Christ. It is no longer I who live, but Christ who lives in me" (Gal. 2:20). To surrender is to give up control of our lives.

Together, these actions are the conscious or intentional acts that give the Holy Spirit freedom to do God's will in our lives:

- Submission: Have you placed your life under the authority of the Lord? Is he the Lord of your life?
- Surrender: Have you given up trying to serve him in your own wisdom and strength? Have you given him control of your life?
- Commitment: Have you agreed to follow the Lord? Has he shown you the path he wants you to take?

"For my thoughts are not your thoughts, neither are your ways my ways, declares the Lord. For as the heavens are higher than the earth, so are my ways higher than your ways and my thoughts than your thoughts" (Isa. 55:8–9).

Perhaps you made this decision to trust in the past but need to refresh that commitment. He stands willing and able to guide and direct your life according to his plan. The following is a suggested prayer of commitment:

Father, I need You. I acknowledge that I have been in control of my life and, as a result, I have sinned against you. Thank you for forgiving my sins through Christ's death on the cross. I now invite Christ to take control of my life. Thank you for placing your Spirit in me. I now yield control of my life to you. Mold me to become Christ to the world to which you have called me. As an expression of my faith, I now thank You for taking control of my life and placing the Holy Spirit in me.[35]

This is what the Lord said will happen when we transfer control of our lives to Him:

I will sprinkle clean water on you, and you shall be clean from all your uncleannesses, and from all your idols I will cleanse you. And I will give you a new heart, and a new spirit I will put within you. And I will remove the heart of stone from your flesh and give you a heart of flesh. And I will put my Spirit within you, and cause you to walk in my statutes and be careful to obey my rules. You shall dwell in the land that I gave to your fathers, and you shall be my people, and I will be your God (Ezek. 36:25–28).

Have you experienced the abundant life provided by Christ in me?

Christ in me: transferring trust.

The benefits of Christ in me:

- I walk in him, rooted and built up, established in the faith, and abounding in thanksgiving (Col. 2:6–7).
- I stand firm in the Lord (Phil. 4:1).
- I am led in triumphant victory (2 Cor. 2:14).
- I am steadfast, immovable, always abounding in the work of the Lord, knowing that in the Lord, my labor is not in vain (1 Cor. 15:58).
- I can do all things through him who strengthens me (Phil. 4:13).
- I have everything I need (Phil. 4:19).
- I rejoice in the Lord always (Phil. 4:4).
- I am being purified (1 John 3:3).
- I am strengthened in him (2 Tim. 2:1).
- I am faithful (Eph. 1:1).
- I have overflowing faith and love (1 Tim. 1:14).
- I am empowered to encourage believers to become mature in him (Col. 1:28).

Christ in me: the abundant life.

Empowered Commitment

THE DEEPER LIFE

You, however, are not in the flesh but in the Spirit, if in fact the Spirit of God dwells in you. Anyone who does not have the Spirit of Christ does not belong to him. But if Christ is in you, although the body is dead because of sin, the Spirit is life because of righteousness. If the Spirit of him who raised Jesus from the dead dwells in you, he who raised Christ Jesus from the dead will also give life to your mortal bodies through his Spirit who dwells in you (Rom. 8:9–11).

CHRIST IN ME

> "But whoever keeps his word, in him truly the love of God is perfected. By this we may know that we are in him: whoever says he abides in him ought to walk in the same way in which he walked" (1 John 2:5–6).

*H*ow much freedom do we give the Holy Spirit in us. how much control do we give the him? Have we experienced the power of the Spirit working in and through us? What are the benefits of unleashing the Spirit?

As believers, we often hold God at arm's length, either consciously or subconsciously. When we do this, we limit the power of Christ in me. We become a dam holding the Spirit back. This impedes our growth, limits promised blessings, and inhibits our service to others. The Spirit encourages us to seek a deeper relationship with the Lord. Unfortunately, we often avoid that closer walk with the Lord and fail to experience his power to overcome the challenges and uncertainties of daily living and service to him.

Theologian, Elmer Towns, believes that: "Not everyone who becomes a Christian goes on to live for God, so not every believer experiences a Spirit-filled life. It is an experience that has potential but is not claimed."[36]

Pastor and author A. W. Tozer said that for there to be a deeper life in Christ, there must be a revolt against ordinary faith and an unquenchable hunger to know the "deep, essentially spiritual, and inward power of the Christian message. The deeper life must be understood to mean a life in the Spirit far in advance of the average and nearer to the New Testament norm."[37] Tozer said that we need to have the same spiritual energy, wisdom, and enthusiasm that was in the first century church.

It is only when we experience a profound awareness of our inadequacy that we surrender to the power of God, and we begin to experience the deeper life. Paul said, "Work out your own salvation with fear and trembling, for it is God who works in you, both to will and to work for his good pleasure" (Phil. 2:12b–13).

God is holy and able to demonstrate that holiness through us. His power in us breaks the bonds of sin that we carry from our pre-salvation life. Pardington states that as Christ lives in us and works in us, we experience:

> Far wider and richer things than mere victory over sin, however that victory may be. It includes also the thought of the indwelling Christ, of acute God-consciousness, of rapturous worship, separation from the world, the joyous surrender of everything to God, internal union with the Trinity, the practice of the presence of God, the communion of saints, and prayer without ceasing.[38]

No matter how mature we are, we have only just begun to unleash the power within us.

Tozer defines the deeper life in this way:[39]

- Judicial: An increasingly accountable relationship with the Lord; a sincere acknowledgment that we are in a parent-child relationship with the Lord.
- Vital: A vine-and-branches relationship where we draw life-giving nourishment from the Lord; a receiving of spiritual nourishment.
- Volitional: An awareness of the path on which God has placed us and a conscious willingness, a deliberate choice, to follow that path.
- Intellectual: The development of a Christlike mind; being so tuned to the Lord's frequency that we think like him; having the mind of Christ.
- Emotional: A growing, unbridled response to salvation and the person of Jesus who makes it possible; a deep-seated love for the Lord.
- Freedom from earthly loves: A maturing mindset that guards against the glitter of the world; a growing awareness of the world's negative influence.

Have you surrendered to the power of God in you? Are you practicing the presence of God?

Christ in me: total surrender.

THE CRISIS EXPERIENCE

"If we live by the Spirit, let us also keep in step with the Spirit" (Gal. 5:25).

When we make a serious commitment to Christ, there is a growing awareness that "Christ in me" enables us to overcome that which holds us back. For some, as in my case, the spiritual journey moved slower than a glacier. On the other hand, some experience a crisis, a dramatic awareness of the power of the Spirit setting them apart for service in his kingdom early in their journey. Pardington describes it this way:

> Conversion imparts a new spiritual life and takes away the love of sin, but it does not change the old heart nor destroy the power of sin. Conversion alone means constantstruggles andcertaindefeats in warfare withsin and self. Victory is assured only through the reception of the Holy Spirit and the indwelling of the risen Christ. But this involves a new experience, a second definite work of grace—a crisis as radical and revolutionary as the crisis of the new birth. In regeneration, we pass out of death into life; but in sanctification we pass out of the self-life into the Christ-life. In regeneration we receive a "new spirit;" in sanctification we receive the Holy Spirit to indwell the "new spirit."[40]

"You, however, are not in the flesh but in the Spirit, if in fact the Spirit of God dwells in you. Anyone who does not have the Spirit of Christ does not belong to him" (Rom. 8:9). At salvation, we receive all the Holy Spirit we will ever get. As we mature spiritually, we recognize the Spirit's presence more and allow more of him to work in and through us. The crisis experience is a breakthrough. It comes when we understand at a deep level that there are barriers we cannot overcome, patterns of thinking and behaviors that cannot be broken. The path to victory eludes us. The crisis experience is not a third working of the Spirit but a deeper commitment, absolute submission, and total surrender.

Why does it take a crisis to break through into total surrender? Just as Paul faced a crisis on the Damascus Road that brought spiritual transformation (Acts 9:1–19), we encounter mental or behavioral barriers that take us out of the Lord's will. We need transformation. A crisis puts our life into spiritual perspective. Other biblical examples of the crisis experience include:

- Moses at the burning bush met God and was empowered to lead the children of Israel (Exod. 3:1–15).
- Jacob wrestled with the angel in darkness (fear and uncertainty), encountering someone he could not defeat— he had encountered God (Gen. 32:25–33).
- Isaiah, worshiping in the temple, was overwhelmed by the presence of God, heard God's call, and the message he was to speak (Isa. 6:1–13).

The Crisis Experience of Others

C. L. Culpepper, missionary to Shantung, China, in the 1920s, wrote that he came under heavy conviction in response to three questions: Have you been born of the Spirit? What evidence do you have of the new birth? Have you been filled with the Holy Spirit? He wrote that: "The Holy Spirit and God's Word continued to probe until I believed I would die under the searching, accusing finger of God...I told my Chinese co-workers that in their compliments of me as an effective worker, I had stolen God's glory. My heart was so broken I didn't believe I could live any longer."[41]

Theologian Elmer Towns recalls that one morning, as a new believer, he was challenged by the phrase "I live by the faith of the Son of God" in Galatians 2:20. He realized, for the first time, that Christ lived in him, and thus he voluntarily made a renewed commitment to the Lord. He said:

> I asked Jesus Christ to give me victory by living His faith through me. Jesus Christ had never gotten discouraged, and I wanted to live above discouragement. I wanted not only faith that could trust God for money, but also faith that would not worry about anything. I wanted to trust completely in Him. What I experienced was inward reality. I did not kneel in prayer, nor did I dose my eyes. I simply talked to Jesus and yielded everything to Him. I asked Jesus Christ to live His life through me. That morning, for the first time in my Christian life, I fully experienced

the meaning of the resurrection life.[42]

John Wesley's story is similar. He had returned to England from America, disappointed and disillusioned by poor results from his preaching. On May 24, 1738, while listening to someone read Luther's introduction to the book of Romans on the change God works in the heart through faith in Christ, he said his heart was strangely warmed. He reported he had assurance that his sins had been forgiven. Empowered by the Spirit, he went on to a successful ministry.[43]

> "Commit your way to the Lord; trust in him, and he will act. He will bring forth your righteousness as the light, and your justice as the noonday" (Ps. 37:5–6).

My Crisis Experience

In my case, my mediocre spiritual journey was powerfully interrupted. I asked my pastor for accountability. He revealed that I often spoke my mind in ways that were hurtful. I was taken aback. After all, I was just being honest. I saw things that needed to be corrected and spoke my mind. Immediately, the Lord brought things to my mind I had said that were inappropriate. I came under conviction.

More frustrating, however, was that there was no obvious way to correct that behavior. Apparently, it was an engrained pattern of behavior. There was no off switch. How could I control what came out of my mouth? Did I have the self-discipline to screen what came out of my mouth? Should I just stop talking? I was reminded of what James said about the tongue:

> If we put bits into the mouths of horses so that they obey us, we guide their whole bodies as well. Look at the ships also: though they are so large and are driven by strong winds, they are guided by a very small rudder wherever the will of the pilot directs. So also the tongue is a small member, yet it boasts of great things. How great a forest is set ablaze by such a small fire! (James 3:3–5).

I knew my tendency to speak my mind was a matter that needed correction and that I could not make this change on my own, so I laid the matter before the Lord... and then forgot about it. Amazing! He corrected the problem. I still see things that need to be corrected but am restrained in my approach to the problem.

Are you in bondage? Do you need a breakthrough in your calling? Is there a needed behavior change? Is something holding you back? Do you need to experience God working in your life in new ways?

Christ in me: moving beyond ordinary faith.

SPIRITUAL INSIGHT

Knowing Right from Wrong

"But test everything; hold fast what is good" (1 Thess. 5:21).

Now the works of the flesh are evident: sexual immorality, impurity, sensuality, idolatry, sorcery, enmity, strife, jealousy, fits of anger, rivalries, dissensions, divisions, envy, drunkenness, orgies, and things like these. I warn you, as I warned you before, that those who do such things will not inherit the kingdom of God. But the fruit of the Spirit is love, joy, peace, patience, kindness, goodness, faithfulness, gentleness, self-control; against such things there is no law. And those who belong to Christ Jesus have crucified the flesh with its passions and desires (Gal. 5:19–24).

As we allow the Spirit to work in us, he cleans out inappropriate attitudes, behaviors, and speech. Those things that are not pleasing to the Lord begin to disappear. The Spirit working in us is a lifelong process. While salvation makes us right with the Lord, it is the Spirit who cleans us up and sets us apart to be more Christlike.

Then there are those things in our lives that, while not wrong, distract, divert, and hinder us from being effective instruments of the Lord. They are like a dull knife that will cut but not cleanly. They clutter the path forward. For example, I developed an early passion for classic cars and routinely visited several classic car websites. It was a hobby. One day, I mentioned my interest in my Sunday school class. It must have been confession and repentance because several weeks later I realized I did not have a desire to visit those sites. The Lord said, "What you are doing is not wrong. It is just wrong for you." Why? Was it an inappropriate use of time? Was it vain imagination? Would it lead to actions outside his will?

Discerning People's Actions and Motives

> "Now when he was in Jerusalem at the Passover Feast, many believed in his name when they saw the signs that he was doing. But Jesus on his part did not entrust himself to them, because he knew all people and needed no one to bear witness about man, for he himself knew what was in man" (John 2:23–25).

These verses are important in understanding the conversations Jesus had with Nicodemus (John 3:1–21), the Samaritan woman (John 4:5–26), and the official at Cana (John 4:46–53). In each of these cases, Jesus spoke with insight into the spiritual need of each.

While it is easy to accept Jesus's insight into the hearts of people, it is not natural to think that the same spiritual insight is available to us. However, with his Spirit in us, we can have spiritual insight as we interact with others.

Consider Peter dealing with Ananias and Sapphira. He discerned that they had sold their land for more than they claimed. Peter knew they had lied about what they had given.

But a man named Ananias, with his wife Sapphira, sold a piece of property, and with his wife's knowledge he kept back for himself some of the proceeds and brought only a part of it and laid it at the apostles' feet. But Peter said, "Ananias, why has Satan filled your heart to lie to the Holy Spirit and to keep back for yourself part of the proceeds of the land?" (Acts 5:1–3).

We may not recognize these moments as discernment, but there are times we inherently know what to say or the Scripture to use in a situation.

Appropriate Words

Consider spiritual gifts: encouragement, exhortation, evangelism, and teaching to name a few. In each case, the Holy Spirit puts thoughts in our minds, words in our mouths, and motivates us to act as we engage with believers and non-believers. Spiritual insight comes with true and continuing surrender to the power of the Holy Spirit. This insight comes with a sincere belief that we are empowered to minister to others. It comes with time in the Word. It comes through a regular prayer life in which the Lord directs our relationships. He brings an eternal perspective. We need to bathe each visit, each conversation in prayer.

A believer may not be aware of spiritual insight. The Holy Spirit may use us merely by our presence or a word or phrase. At times it is thoughts or words that come, and we wonder, "Where did that come from?"

"Whoever believes in me, as the Scripture has said, 'Out of his heart will flow rivers of living water'" (John 7:38).

I am amazed when teaching, sharing, or just engaging in conversation, needed words come that are not from me. I find myself encouraging others when I do not have a clue what I am doing. God is working through me.

Spiritual Ears

> "Call to me and I will answer you, and will tell you great and hidden things that you have not known" (Jer. 33:3).

> "Christ in me" helps us hear the Lord on his terms, not in human terms. Here are some examples from the gospel of John.

Nicodemus (John 3:1–15). Jesus: "Unless one is born again [spiritual birth], he cannot see the kingdom of God." Nicodemus: "How can a man be born [physical birth], when he is old?" It is natural that Nicodemus missed what Jesus was saying. Nicodemus believed that keeping the law and the prophets brought him into communion with God. He believed that he could achieve eternal life by works. Jesus was calling him to a belief system that depends on the Spirit, that is, being born from above.

The Woman at the well (John 4:10–11, 19–25). Jesus: "You would have asked him, and he would have given you living water" (spiritual water essential for spiritual life). Woman: "Sir, you have nothing to draw water with" (physical water for physical life). She asked Jesus to give her living water so that she would not have to come and draw water from the well. Perceiving Jesus to be a prophet, she asked him about the proper place for worship, thinking in physical terms. Jesus told her that God was a spirit and should be worshiped in spirit.

The crowd (John 6:34–35). Crowd: "Give us this bread always" (physical bread to sustain physical life). Jesus: "I am the bread of life" (spiritual bread to sustain spiritual life). Like the woman at the well, the crowd was thinking about the physical life. Jesus was talking about spiritual food that satisfies the spiritual longing of our souls. By trusting in Jesus, the longing to know God will be satisfied. The soul is satisfied only when we rest in God.

Mary, sister of Lazarus (John 11:23–24). Jesus: "Your brother will rise again" (be restored to physical life). Mary: "I know he will rise again" (eternal life after death, the resurrection of the soul). Here, the thinking is reversed. Jesus was promising to restore Lazarus to life that day. Mary failed to recognize that Jesus was promising the abundant life now, the personal presence and power of God in daily life.

Thomas (John 14:1–7). Thomas: "How can we know the way?" (the physical path to where Jesus was going). Jesus: "I am the way the truth and the life" (the spiritual path to eternal life—today and after death). Thomas thought Jesus was going to an earthly location, perhaps to establish an earthly kingdom. This was a heart cry. Thomas wanted to be with Jesus. He could not understand why he could not go where Jesus was going. The path we are on is spiritual, and we are guided by "Christ in me."

Philip (John 14:8–9). Philip: "Show us the Father" (seeking something he could see, touch, or hear). Jesus: "Whoever has seen me has seen the Father" (Emmanuel—God with us). Philip's request is closely related to that of Thomas's: "Let us see God." It is difficult for us to believe in something we cannot see. This is the position of atheists and agnostics. We can, however, experience the presence of God in our lives and see his presence in the lives of others. We see him present in transformed lives, healing, scriptural insight, creation, and the like. These insights come from the indwelling Spirit.

To hear the Lord, we need to use our "Christ in me" spiritual ears.

Spiritual Eyes

> "I tell you, lift up your eyes, and see that the fields are
> white for harvest" (John 4:35).

"Christ in me" opens our eyes to see the path the Lord has for us and the opportunities he places before us. With "Christ in me," we see:

- Those who need salvation
- Those who need encouragement
- Those who need exhortation
- Those who need compassion
- Those who need to hear the truth
- Those who need healing
- Those who have physical needs

We are designed and empowered to make a difference in the lives of others. Spiritual eyes, ears, and mindsets enable us to be Christ to those we encounter.

Insight into the Word

"For the word of God is living and active, sharper than any two-edged sword, piercing to the division of soul and of spirit, of joints and of marrow, and discerning the thoughts and intentions of the heart" (Heb. 4:12).

"All Scripture is breathed out by God and profitable for teaching, for reproof, for correction, and for training in righteousness, that the man of God may be complete, equipped for every good work" (2 Tim. 3:16–17).

"Your word is a lamp to my feet and a light to my path" (Ps. 119:105).

"Everyone then who hears these words of mine and does them will be like a wise man who built his house on the rock" (Matt. 7:24).

"But he answered, 'It is written, "Man shall not live by bread alone, but by every word that comes from the mouth of God"'" (Matt. 4:4).

"Whoever believes in me, as the Scripture has said, 'Out of his heart will flow rivers of living water'" (John 7:38).

Do you see, hear, and think in spiritual terms?

Christ in me: spiritual insight.

THE DISAPPEARING ME

John the Baptist said: "He must increase, but I must decrease" (John 3:30).

"I have been crucified with Christ. It is no longer I who live, but Christ who lives in me. And the life I now live in the flesh I live by faith in the Son of God, who loved me and gave himself for me" (Gal. 2:20).

We want to feel important and valued. We look to the world or others to tell us we are significant or appreciated. Yet the world does not always respond in the way we want, nor is the world consistent in how it responds to us. However, Scripture tells us that we are of value to God and that he accepts us.

Genesis 1:26 says we have been created in the image of God, that we are an undeniable part of his plan, and that our very existence is not the result of a whim, afterthought, or chance. God's action in creating us was purposeful and intentional, a conscious act of God. Therefore, we are of value to God. Our very existence is personal to him. David said, "For you formed my inward parts; you knitted me together in my mother's womb. I praise you, for I am fearfully and wonderfully made" (Ps. 139:13–14).

We are of such value to him that he died for us. He breathed life into our physical bodies, and then, by accepting his sacrifice for us, he breathes spiritual life into us. Jesus was very clear when he said: "Fear not, therefore; you are of more value than many sparrows" (Matt. 10:31). We are significant in God's eyes.

Not only are we unique in the sight of God, but he chose us to be a part of his family. By his own action we are brought into his family and are valued members of that family.

> "In love he predestined us for adoption to himself as sons through Jesus Christ, according to the purpose of his will, to the praise of his glorious grace, with which he has blessed us in the Beloved" (Eph. 1:5–6).

As part of his family, we are called to advance his kingdom. He has called us to proclaim the gospel by our actions and words. He chose us to serve others and minister to their needs. He has chosen us to be leaven in an unbelieving society. "And he said to them, 'Follow me, and I will make you fishers of men'" (Matt. 4:19). Jesus's last command was to:

> "Go therefore and make disciples of all nations, baptizing them in the name of the Father and of the Son and of the Holy Spirit, teaching them to observe all that I have commanded you. And behold, I am with you always, to the end of the age" (Matt. 28:19–20).

The Lord has a purpose or mission for us. More importantly, he has equipped us with the power that raised Jesus from the dead to accomplish that mission (Rom. 8:9–11). The challenge is to measure our importance or value on his terms, not the world's. Because the power of God lives in us, it is he who does the work to carry out his plan.

Therefore, as we mature spiritually, our perceived importance diminishes. As Paul states, "It is no longer I who live but Christ who lives in me" (Gal. 2:20). Anything we do that is of eternal value is done by the Lord. The Holy Spirit is God's hand in my glove working to make a difference in the lives of others. It is the Spirit who is the helium in our balloons. He causes us to rise above our self-interests and move beyond a worldly focus. It is the Spirit who empowers us to carry out the tasks He gives us.

While Scripture indicates that we are important, we are important only as the Lord's instrument in advancing his kingdom. It is not I but Christ in me. To be effective, I must decrease. "Christ in me" must increase. If I am anything, the Lord is not everything.

Do you see yourself as God sees you, as a person of great value to him? Do you measure your value as the world does or in terms of the freedom he has working in and through you?

German pastor, theologian, and martyr Dietrich Bonhoeffer said, "When Christ calls a man, he bids him come and die." [44]

Christ in me: the disappearing me.

FREEDOM

"All your lives you've let sin tell you what to do. But thank God you've started listening to a new master, one whose commands set you free to live openly in his freedom!" (Rom. 6:17–18 MSG). Spiritual transformation moves us from being captive to our own wisdom and will to having freedom in Christ.

Many years ago I was sitting in a Sunday school class where the discussion was on freedom. After several members had given their definitions, Olen Taylor, an older man in the class, offered this: "Freedom is not having to worry about boundaries." He was very clear and confident in his response. I was troubled by this thought. Did he mean we had the freedom to do anything we wanted?

Christ gives us the freedom to choose; to choose to sin, to wander outside his boundaries. Was that the freedom Olen was describing? It took me several years to come to grips with the concept of "not having to worry about the boundaries."

King David defined the boundaries the Lord has established for our lives this way in Psalm 19:7-9:

- The law of the Lord is perfect, converting the soul.
- The testimony of the Lord is sure, making wise the simple.
- The statutes of the Lord are right, rejoicing the heart.
- The commandment of the Lord is pure, enlightening the eyes.
- The fear of the Lord is clean, enduring forever.
- The judgments of the Lord are true and righteous altogether.

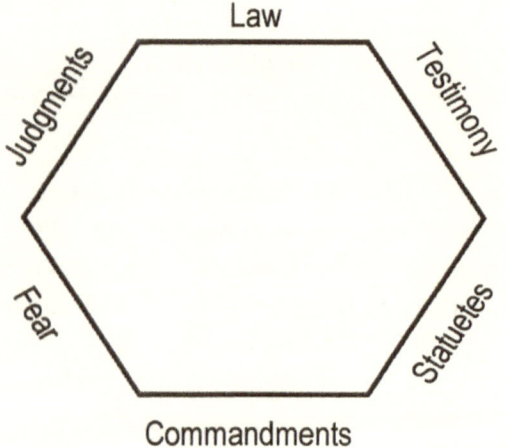

Figure 2. Spiritual Boundaries

As the Lord cleans up our lives, these boundaries, through the power of the Holy Spirit, move us toward Christlike behavior, thoughts, and speech. By that power, our lives increasingly glorify God. We begin to live life without having to worry about crossing his boundaries.

Is the Spirit keeping you inside God's boundaries? Do you have freedom in Christ?

Christ in me: I am set free.

KNOWING AND DOING GOD'S CALL

"Not that I have already attained, or am already perfected; but I press on, that I may lay hold of that for which Christ Jesus has also laid hold of me" (Col. 3:12).

Where do we fit in God's disciple making plan?

Dr. Os Guinness states: "God calls us so decisively in Christ that everything we are, everything we have, and everything we do is invested with a direction and a dynamism because it is done in response to his summons and his call."[45] Guinness suggests that in our Western society, we have failed to define the meaning of the individual life. And "yet there is a deep yearning today for purpose, and yet enormous ignorance and confusion in terms of how we discover it."[46]

There are many examples in Scripture of God calling his servants:

- Moses at the burning bush—to lead the people to the promised land (Exod. 3)
- Gideon while working—to lead the fight against the Midianites (Judg. 6)
- Samuel while asleep—to be a prophet (1 Sam. 3)The Deeper Life
- Isaiah while worshiping—to prophesy (Isa. 6)
- Paul on the Damascus road—to plant churches and make disciples (Acts 9)

In each case, the method of the call and the task given was different. Regardless, God communicated with these men individually and uniquely with a specific command to serve. God calls us through our quiet time, his Word, worship, other believers, and by engaging in service to him. As we move forward with "Christ in me," we gain insight into our spiritual strengths and weaknesses. How do people respond to us? Are they encouraged? Is their faith strengthened? Are they motivated to engage in ministry to others? Do we bring order out of confusion? As Guinness said, "God normally calls us along the line of our giftedness, but the purpose of that giftedness is stewardship and service, not selfishness."[47]

Our call may be contrary to what we think we can do. We may tell the Lord, "I can't do that," and we are right! The Lord calls us not to work in our own wisdom and strength but to allow him to do the work. What is your passion? What motivates you in ministry? Is it teaching, administration, encouraging, exhorting, or helping? Do you experience the supernatural hand of God when you are serving him? What do people say about your gift or gifts? We will address spiritual gifts in the next chapter.

We cannot claim credit for our calling. It is something God places on us. Our calling is something we discover. It is the Spirit within that reveals God's unique purpose for us. It is the Spirit who motivates us, keeps us on track, and energizes us despite distractions and obstacles. Remember Paul's motivation in going to Damascus was to root out Christians, to eliminate the church. Clearly, it was not a call of God. It was something he determined. After his Damascus Road experience, the Spirit took that energy and determination and used it to plant churches and make disciples. In the deeper life, like Paul, we are compelled to advance his kingdom.

> Not that I have already attained, or am already perfected; but I press on, that I may lay hold of that for which Christ Jesus has also laid hold of me. Brethren, I do not count myself to have apprehended; but one thing *I do*, forgetting those things which are behind and reaching forward to those things which are ahead, I press toward the goal for the prize of the upward call of God in Christ Jesus (Col. 3:12–14).

Again, to the Philippians, he wrote:

> "Brothers, I do not consider that I have made it my own. But one thing I do: forgetting what lies behind and straining forward to what lies ahead, I press on toward the goal for the prize of the upward call of God in Christ Jesus" (Phil. 3:13–14 NET).

Having been seized by God, Paul always looked ahead. He set aside those things that interfered with the pursuit of his God-given goal. We are to keep the call of God constantly in front of us. We are to advance like the plowman who looks to the mark at the end of the field. "Christ in me" guides me.

What is God's purpose for your life? What is your calling? Are you on the path God has set for you?

Christ in me: the passion to advance his kingdom.

SUCCESS

Jesus answered, "The most important is, 'Hear, O Israel: The Lord our God, the Lord is one. And you shall love the Lord your God with all your heart and with all your soul and with all your mind and with all your strength.' The second is this: 'You shall love your neighbor as yourself.' There is no other commandment greater than these" (Mark 12:30–31).

The cultural definition of success is the degree or measure of succeeding, a favorable or desired outcome, the attainment of wealth, favor, or eminence.[48] In the above verses, Jesus defined success in terms of the quality of one's relationship with the Lord and with others. He also defined it in terms of being productive, that is, making disciples (John 15:5; Matt. 28:18–20). In other words, obedience.

It is in our DNA to be productive. We have a desire to be successful. How do we define productivity and success? Is it by position, power, and possession? Is it by what others think or what our culture considers important? Or is it in terms of his or her relationship with the Lord, hearing his call and responding? Is it in terms of our relationship with our neighbors? Is it in terms of allowing the Spirit to work in and through us?

After three years of following Jesus and observing him in ministry,

Jesus gave the disciples authority to make disciples. They were commanded to go and be productive in making disciples (Matt. 28:18–20).

Jesus's command came with a promise: "I am with you always, even to the end of the age" (Matt. 28:20). Note that this command is issued in the present tense. "I am..." Jesus did not leave us on our own. He empowers us to do his work, to make disciples. Success comes when we understand that he makes disciples, not us; he is the master disciple maker.

A disciple's focus is on God and others. We need to have our "ears on" to hear those to whom the Lord sends us. He calls some to plant the seed, some to water, some to till the soil, and some to harvest the crop. It is the Holy Spirit who prepares the heart and then does the actual work of salvation, repentance, conversion, and transformation. He is not only with us; he is in us.

- He commands us to make disciples (Matt. 28:18–20).
- He equips us to make disciples (Matt. 12:18).
- He empowers us to make disciples (Act 1:8).
- He works through us to make disciples (Phil. 2:13).

Paul defines success as follows:

Indeed, I count everything as loss because of the surpassing worth of knowing Christ Jesus my Lord. For his sake I have suffered the loss of all things and count them as rubbish, in order that I may gain Christ and be found in him, not having a righteousness of my own that comes from the law, but that which comes through faith in Christ, the righteousness from God that depends on faith— that I may know him and the power of his resurrection, and may share his sufferings, becoming like him in his death, that by any means possible I may attain the resurrection from the dead (Phil. 3:8–11).

And:

Not that I have already obtained this or am already
perfect, but I press on to make it my own, because
Christ Jesus has made me his own. Brothers, I do not
consider that I have made it my own. But one thing I
do: forgetting what lies behind and straining forward to
what lies ahead, I press on toward the goal for the prize
of the upward call of God in Christ Jesus. Let those of
us who are mature think this way, and if in anything
you think otherwise, God will reveal that also to you.
Only let us hold true to what we have attained (Phil.
3:12–17).

Paul set aside the world's measure of success. He rejected the idea of
success based on keeping the law. He understood that success came from
Christ in him. He was empowered to succeed by the Holy Spirit.

"But whoever does what is true comes to the light, so that it may
be clearly seen that his works have been carried out in God" (John
3:21). Jesus said that the deeds of disciples are good because they are
done in the strength and power of God. As believers, we are to
operate in the power of the Spirit. God provides moment-by-moment
direction. When God provided water for the Israelites, he used a
different method each time (Exod. 15:22–27; 17:1–7). The Lord's
strategy for conquering Ai was different from that of conquering
Jericho (Josh. 5:13–6:23; 7:1–26). When Jesus healed the blind, he used
a different method each time. What makes us think that the way he
worked in the past will be the way he works today? Therefore, we must
depend on God in us to carry out his work.

"I can do **all things** through Christ who strengthens
me" (Phil. 4:13, emphasis added).

How do you define success? Is it on your terms or his?

Christ in me: achieving success on his terms.

CONTENTMENT

> "Not that I am speaking of being in need, for I have learned in whatever situation I am to be content. I know how to be brought low, and I know how to abound. In any and every circumstance, I have learned the secret of facing plenty and hunger, abundance and need. I can do all things through him who strengthens me" (Phil. 4:11–13).

Contentment is to be free from concern because of satisfaction with what is already one's own. The Hebrew word simply means "to be pleased." Contentment is an inward sense of satisfaction; discontentment is a habit or state of mind that has to do with focus, occurrence, or object.[49] Contentment means being satisfied with who we are, where we are, what we are doing, and what we have.

I know I am his. Contentment is knowing whose I am rather than who I am. Contentment comes from knowing that we are unique in the eyes of God and that he has a specific plan for us. Discontentment comes from trying to be something other than what God intended. Who am I? I am a part of God's family and am empowered by God to serve him. Contentment is knowing I am his.

> "For in Christ Jesus you are all sons of God, through faith" (Gal. 3:26).

> "And because you are sons, God has sent the Spirit of his Son into our hearts, crying, "Abba! Father!" So you are no longer a slave, but a son, and if a son, then an heir through God" (Gal. 4:6–7).

I am where I need to be. Contentment is being where God wants me. We operate based on calendars and clocks. We know where we need to be and what time we need to be there. Contentment is knowing that the calendar and clock of my life are directed by God.

Geographically: Jesus sent his disciples to Jerusalem, Judea, Samaria, and the world. Where is God sending you? Is he sending you to a person, neighborhood, region, or another country? Contentment is being where God has called you.

Positionally: We are called to a personal relationship with the Lord. That relationship grows as we mature. When our earthly life is over, we will stand perfect before the Lord. Until that time, we must allow the Spirit to continue transforming us into servants useful to the Lord. We must never become complacent with who and where we are with him. Contentment is being in Christ and knowing "Christ in me."

I am doing what I need to do. Contentment is spending time in your God-given passion. It is knowing that God is working through you. Discontentment is operating based on your own wisdom and understanding. My passion is administration. My challenge is that I become so focused on my work that I forget that I am also called to disciple others—building his kingdom. I am an introvert. I tend to hide in my grace gift. I must guard against the desire to retreat into my passion and not have time for others. "Let each of you look not only to his own interests, but also to the interests of others" (Phil. 2:4). Contentment is knowing and doing God's calling.

> "And let us not grow weary of doing good, for in due season we will reap, if we do not give up. So then, as we have opportunity, let us do good to everyone, and especially to those who are of the household of faith" (Gal. 6:9).

I am satisfied with what I have. Contentment is knowing that God will provide all our needs. Discontentment is being distracted by things of the world. Often the things we possess are beyond what we need and they, in turn, possess us. A coworker once shared that his first car gave him continuous trouble. His grandmother asked, "Who does the car belong to, you or the Lord?" Contentment is knowing the difference between needs and wants. Contentment is knowing that all we have comes from God and is on loan to us.

Discontentment is striving to grasp those things that are not in God's plan for us. "Keep your life free from love of money, and be content with what you have, for he has said, 'I will never leave you nor forsake you'" (Heb. 13:5). And "Seek first the kingdom of God and his righteousness, and all these things will be added to you" (Matt. 6:33).

> "But whatever gain I had, I counted as loss for the sake of Christ. Indeed, I count everything as loss because of the surpassing worth of knowing Christ Jesus my Lord. For his sake I have suffered the loss of all things and count them as rubbish, in order that I may gain Christ and be found in him..." (Phil. 3:7–9).

> But the day of the Lord will come like a thief, and then the heavens will pass away with a roar, and the heavenly bodies will be burned up ... the heavens will be set on fire and dissolved, and the heavenly bodies will melt as they burn! But according to his promise we are waiting for new heavens and a new earth in which righteousness dwells (2 Pet. 3:10, 12–13).

Paul defined his contentment in terms of his relationship with Christ, not material possessions. We know that all Paul owned he carried on his back. He knew he did not need anything more. Peter used the end times as a measure of contentment. Only what is left is of eternal value. Does what we have contribute to his kingdom?

Do we need anything more? Contentment is knowing the difference between needs and wants.

Are you content with who you are, where you are, and what you have?

Christ in me: contentment.

PASSION

"Don't burn out; keep yourselves fueled and aflame. Be alert servants of the Master, cheerfully expectant. Don't quit in hard times; pray all the harder. Help needy Christians; be inventive in hospitality" (Rom. 12:11–13 MSG).

Dog mushing is the state sport of Alaska. Each musher has thirty or more dogs. Each day the mushers exercise their dogs. When it is time to exercise the dogs, the dogs leap onto their coops and bark vigorously. That barking continues until a team of eight or ten is harnessed, then those left jump down and wait for the next group to be exercised. The barking is an attempt to get the musher to choose them. The point is that sled dogs are bred to race or pull loads over long distances. Running is their life, and they eagerly seek an opportunity to work or race.

We are saved and empowered to serve the Master. We are energized to advance his kingdom. Like sled dogs, we need to pursue God's plan with passion. We can fervently be engaged in the work of the Lord because we are empowered by His Spirit.

"Truly, truly, I say to you, whoever believes in me will also do the works that I do; and greater works than these will he do, because I am going to the Father.

Whatever you ask in my name, this I will do, that the Father may be glorified in the Son. If you ask me anything in my name, I will do it" (John 14:12–14).

"O God, you are my God; earnestly I seek you; my soul thirsts for you; my flesh faints for you, as in a dry and weary land where there is no water" (Ps. 63:1).

"My soul longs, yes, faints for the courts of the Lord; my heart and flesh sing for joy to the living God" (Ps. 84:2).

Our spiritual energy or passion comes in many forms as the Lord uniquely equips us and positions us for advancing his kingdom. Being energized for service does not necessarily mean physical energy. It is a deep desire to be used by God in whatever situation or circumstance he has placed us. The deeper life is a life of passion for the person and work of the Lord.

Do you have a passion for serving the Lord? Are you passionate about seeing lives changed?

Christ in me: the passionate pursuit of his calling.

THE DEEPER LIFE

Don't even run little errands that are connected with that old way of life. Throw yourselves wholeheartedly and full-time (remember, you've been raised from the dead!) into God's way of doing things. Sin can't tell you how to live. After all, you're not living under that old tyranny any longer. You're living in the freedom of God (Rom. 6:13–14 MSG).

The Challenge of Life in the Spirit

Towns states that: "The deeper Christian life is described in various terms (*the abiding life, the victorious life*, and so on), it is ultimately a life characterized by seeking God and walking with him. It is a life lived in relationship to God and at the heart of this relationship is the believer's seeking God or the surrender to God."[50] Towns continues by defining two aspects of surrender: "The deeper life is a matter of surrender... There is the initial surrender (once for all). This is the surrender to the ownership of God. The second is daily surrender for guidance."[51]

Oswald Chambers, author of *My Utmost for His Highest*, states: "Surrender is not the surrender of eternal life, but the will; when that is done. The great crisis is the surrender of the will. God never crushes a man's will into surrender, He never beeches him, He waits until man yields up his will to him. That battle never needs to be re-fought."[52]

The deeper life comes from a Spirit-inspired, profound desire to be a living sacrifice, to be under God's authority, to be completely surrendered. Pardington summarizes the experience of the deeper life:

> Beloved, have you received the Holy Ghost? Have you taken Christ to be your sanctification? Have you had a vision of the world's need? Has there come to you the outward calling? If so, then you are living an unselfish life. Then you are bringing forth fruit unto God. Then you are burning with missionary zeal. If so, then you have a passion for souls. Then you love the lost and are seeking to save them. Then you are pressed in spirit towards "the regions beyond." Surely, you will go, if you can. Surely, you will give what you can. Surely, you will pray all you can.[53]

The Deeper Life

Christ in Me
The Crisis
Experience
Spiritual Insight
Disappearing Me
Freedom
Set Free
Success
Contentment
Passion

The deeper life comes from an intense understanding that the life we are to live comes not from us, but from the Holy Spirit in us. It is a recognition that when God calls us to a task, ministry, or need, he will do that work. The deeper life comes out of a struggle, a crisis, when we concede that we cannot do the work of the Lord on our own. It is a heartfelt surrender, not just a mental agreement. The deeper life comes with an unquenchable burden.

The Anglican priest and theologian, John Stott, wrote, "Christians should be eager to develop their gifts, widen their opportunities, extend their influence and be given promotion in their work—not now to boost their own ego or build their own empire, but rather through everything they do to bring glory to God."[54]

It is one thing to have hold of the Lord but quite another for him to have hold of us. Holding onto him brings his peace in times of challenge and uncertainty. Allowing him to have hold of us takes us where he calls, when he calls, and do what he wants.

Salvation comes through the leading of the Holy Spirit in convicting of sin, righteousness, and judgment (John16:8). Spiritual transformation comes through transferring control of one's life to the Spirit and acknowledging that the Spirit is ready, willing, and able to make us Christlike. The deeper life comes through a Spirit-inspired, overwhelming, deep-seated desire to walk with and serve the Lord.

Table 2. Salvation, Commitment, and the Deeper Life

Decision	Holy Spirit	Motivation	Result
Salvation	Conviction: sin, righteousness, and judgment	I am a sinner and cannot save myself.	Assurance of salvation and the indwelling Spirit
Commitment	Conviction: the need to surrender to the Lord	I cannot live the Christian life.	Transformation in living and service to the Lord
Deeper Life	Conviction: the need to be completely committed	I am not who God has called me to be.	A fresh openness to be used by the Lord

The deeper life is not a new filling of the Spirit. It is the already present Spirit urging us to seek a more serious relationship with the Lord and be willing to go whenever and wherever the Lord asks and do whatever he asks. The deeper life is a commitment on steroids.

Praying for the Deeper Life

While there are suggested prayers for salvation and commitment, praying for deeper life flows from a personal and overpowering desire to live and work beyond one's wisdom and strength, unleash the power of the Spirit within, and be completely surrendered to the Lord. This desire is Spirit-driven. Therefore, the prayer for a deeper life is Spirit-enabled, and the words prayed come from the Spirit. They come from "Christ in me."

> And so, from the day we heard, we have not ceased to pray for you, asking that you may be filled with the knowledge of his will in all spiritual wisdom and understanding, so as to walk in a manner worthy of the Lord, fully pleasing to him: bearing fruit in every good work and increasing in the knowledge of God; being strengthened with all power, according to his glorious might, for all endurance and patience with joy; giving thanks to the Father, who has qualified you to share in the inheritance of the saints in light (Col. 1:9–12).

Are you giving the Lord total freedom to work in and through you? Have you given the Lord total control of your life?

Christ in me: empowered commitment.

Empowered Service

SPIRITUAL GIFTS

"Now there are varieties of gifts, but the same Spirit; and there are varieties of service, but the same Lord; and there are varieties of activities, but it is the same God who empowers them all in everyone. To each is given the manifestation of the Spirit for the common good" (1 Cor. 12:4–7).

INTRODUCTION55

*H*aving delt with salvation, spiritual transformation, and the deeper life, we now move on to tools that God gives us for effective service in ministry to others and building his kingdom, spiritual gifts (*charisma*).

Spiritual Gifts

Spiritual gifts are the active presence of the Spirit who flows or works through each believer uniquely. Spiritual gifts are the Spirit at work using our mind, eyes, ears, hands, heart, and feet to advance his kingdom as God determines. The effective outpouring of spiritual gifts depends on the openness of the believer to be used by the Spirit and the acceptance by the person on the receiving end.

Spiritual Gifts and the Body of Christ

Each time Paul addressed spiritual gifts, he did so in terms of the body of Christ. He specified that the gifts given to individuals are to be used for the effective functioning and operation of the body (Rom. 12:4–6). He stressed that spiritual gifts are to be used for strengthening the faith of the body, that is, helping the body achieve spiritual transformation or maturity (Eph. 4:12–16). Then in 1 Corinthians 12, Paul lays out two lists in his most passionate discussion of the relationship between spiritual gifts and the body. He urges believers to view the church as having many parts (believers), with each applying their own gift and working together effectively to advance the kingdom.

Paul urged believers to view spiritual gifts not as possessions or badges. Instead, gifts are tools essential for expanding the kingdom in Jerusalem, Judea, Samaria, and to the ends of the earth. After all, a spiritual gift is God at work in and through us to do the work he directs. Spiritual gifts are to be viewed through the lens of the church, its members individually, and the body as a whole. Paul cautions believers not to elevate one person or gift over another in the functioning of the body (Rom. 12:3; 1 Cor. 12:21–26). However, he does specify that the church "desire" the gifts of apostle, prophet, and teacher as essential in transforming individuals and the body (1 Cor. 12:31). God is glorified when spiritual gifts are exercised.

The Giver of the Gifts

Spiritual gifts involve all three members of the Trinity. All spiritual gifts were determined by God before creation. Before he did anything, he decided everything (Eph. 1:3–10). He determined what gifts each believer will receive, when they are to be given, and how they are to be used. Therefore, God is the source of spiritual gifts. God, however, has given Jesus authority over the church and the ability to provide gifts to the body. In turn, Jesus sent the Holy Spirit who does his (Jesus's) bidding. It is the Holy Spirit who empowers believers toward service (John 16:5–16). Thus, we see the Trinity working in harmony with the body.

Understanding Spiritual Gifts

The challenge for us is to understand the diversity of the gifts, which ones we have received, and when and where we are to apply them. Adding to these challenges, Pauzl provides four lists in his letter to the churches in Rome, Ephesus, and Corinth. The letters were to two churches he knew well (the Ephesian and Corinthian churches) and one he knew little about (the church in Rome). His purpose for writing each letter was different as the conditions in each church were different. Therefore, the context is important in understanding each list. We will discuss these differences as we look at each list. As the four lists differ, some believe they are only a sampling of the gifts available.[56] For our purposes, we will consider the lists to be complete because Paul addresses different gifts and a single purpose in each list.

The Kinds of Spiritual Gifts, Services, and Workings

We will begin our discussion of spiritual gifts with 1 Corinthians 12. Paul said, "Now concerning spiritual gifts, brothers, I do not want you to be uninformed" (1 Cor. 12:1). He then stated:

> "There are different kinds of gifts, but the same Spirit distributes them. There are different kinds of service, but the same Lord. There are different kinds of working, but in all of them and in everyone it is the same God at work. Now to each one the manifestation of the Spirit is given for the common good" (1 Cor. 12:4–7).

Paul used the word, "kinds" as it relates to gifts, services, and workings. In Greek, this word means division, distribution, distinction, or difference.[57]

By applying the above verses to the four lists mentioned above, we can gain insight into Paul's thinking:

There are different kinds of gifts (*charismaton*) but the same Spirit. Spiritual gifts are made real when they are given to each believer as the Spirit chooses. There is to be unity within the rich diversity reflecting the nature of God that is seen in the church.[58]

Paul's four lists are:

- Grace gifts (Rom. 12:6–8)
- Situational or results gifts (1 Cor. 12:7–11)
- Body gifts (1 Cor. 12:28–31)
- Leadership gifts (Eph. 4:10–16)

There are different kinds of service (*diakonion* – plural) but the same Lord. Believers are given gifts to minister to the body as directed by the Lord. Therefore, believers are called to be ready to apply their gifts. Paul's message is that all believers and their gifts are considered equally worthy by the Lord.[59] There are unending possibilities for applying these gifts. For example, various forms of ministry include:

- Administration
- Caring
- Encouraging
- Service to one another

There are different kinds of workings (*energenaton* – plural) but the same God. God works (brings forth results) as believers exercise their gifts when and where the Lord directs. God's power is demonstrated in changed lives, relationships, churches, communities, and the world.[60] Ways in which God works are as follows:

- Permanent
- Temporary
- Multiple
- Depending on obedience

The gifts are given for the common good. The result of applying spiritual gifts in service to the Lord is the public and open demonstration of the power of God for the benefit of the community of believers. The result displays God's attributes in the body, which promotes the common good and glorifies God.[61]

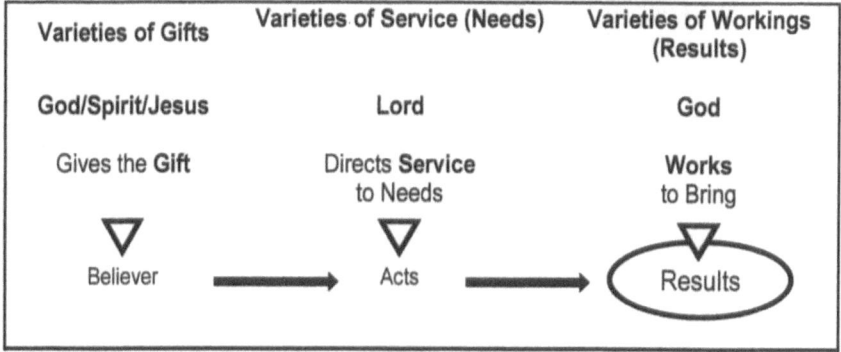

Figure 3. Spiritual Gifts in Action

Have you experienced the Spirit working through you in ways that you know did not come from you?

**Christ in me: supernatural actions that
impact others or the body as a whole.**

GRACE OR MOTIVATIONAL GIFTS

Scripture

> For by the grace given to me I say to everyone among
> you not to think of himself more highly than he ought
> to think, but to think with sober judgment, each
> according to the measure of faith that God has
> assigned. For as in one body we have many members,
> and the members do not all have the same function, so
> we, though many, are one body in Christ, and
> individually members one of another. Having gifts that
> differ according to the **grace** given to us, let us use
> them: if prophecy, in proportion to our faith; if service,
> in our serving; the one who teaches, in his teaching;

the one who exhorts, in his exhortation; the one who contributes, in generosity; the one who leads, with zeal; the one who does acts of mercy, with cheerfulness (Rom. 12:3–8, emphasis added).

"As each [believer] has received a gift, use it to serve one another, as good stewards of God's varied **grace**" (1 Pet. 4:10, emphasis added).

Definition

A grace gift is a supernatural endowment that motivates action in the life of a believer that is given, sustained, and empowered by the Holy Spirit. A grace gift is the Holy Spirit working through an individual to minister to others or the body as a whole.

The Context of the Passage

Romans: Paul's letter to the Roman church presented the basic gospel and doctrine of the Christian faith. This was a church Paul did not know personally; therefore, we have the comprehensive doctrinal nature of the letter. The key element in the letter is the path to righteousness and the work of the Spirit for righteous living. Paul focuses on the doctrine of salvation and its application for holy living. He addresses the two-way communication between God and believer. Of particular importance is the power and role of the Holy Spirit in the life of believers, the unity of the body, and spreading the gospel.

Romans 12: Paul began a new thought in this chapter. His focus here is on righteous living or the practical application of the preceding doctrinal discussion. He began by exhorting the Romans to become living sacrifices, not conforming to the world, and thus being able to determine God's will. He then outlines spiritual gifts that equip believers to uniquely serve the body of Christ. He challenged the Roman church to be humble and recognize that each member is a part of one body without regard to the spiritual gift each believer possessed.

Giver of the Gifts

The consensus among Bible scholars is that God is the giver of grace gifts. This thinking is based on verses three and six, where God is the giver of grace and faith and therefore grace gifts.[62] On the other hand, G. R. Osborn takes a trinitarian approach because Paul stated that the Spirit is the giver of situation gifts (1 Cor. 12:7–11). God is the giver of body gifts (1 Cor. 12:28–31), and Jesus is the giver of leadership gifts (Eph. 4:11). Moreover, Ken Boa and W. Krudnier consider the giver of grace gifts to be the Holy Spirit.[63]

The Nature of the Gifts

God gives each believer a grace gift, that is, "If a man's gift is..." (singular). He told the Corinthians "one has this gift, another has that..." (1 Cor. 7:7). Grace gifts are the focus, framework, mindset, or motivating factor in the believer's life. They are given by grace and empowered based on the level of one's faith and may vary by individual and the gift. The gift given to us has nothing to do with our character or length of service.[64] The words "they are given" in the Greek indicate that these gifts are permanent. We see the evidence in the lives of believers by their actions. Paul indicates that believers, using their grace gifts, complete the body.

> For by the grace given to me I say to everyone among you not to think of himself more highly than he ought to think, but to think with sober judgment, each according to the measure of faith that God has assigned. For as in one body we have many members, and the members do not all have the same function, so we, though many, are one body in Christ, and individually members of one another (Rom. 12:3–5).

Peter said this about grace gifts:

> As each has received a gift, use it to serve one another, as good stewards of God's varied grace: whoever speaks,

as one who speaks oracles of God; whoever serves, as
one who serves by the strength that God supplies—in
order that in everything God may be glorified through
Jesus Christ. To him belong glory and dominion forever
and ever. Amen (1 Pet. 4:10–11).

One's grace gift is how he or she operates in the body of Christ.
We are given natural abilities at physical birth and spiritual gifts at
spiritual birth. Grace gifts are our central motivation for service. They
are a life message. We see and respond to the needs of the body in
terms of our gift. We are vessels to be used by the Holy Spirit.

The Gifts

Prophecy (propheteia)[65] — the Spirit-directed power to reveal
God's truth to the church. Old Testament prophets spoke the truth
(forth-telling) and predicted the future (foretelling). From the New
Testament perspective, prophecy is the divinely inspired
proclamation of truth. Some believe the prophets were itinerant
preachers who moved from church to church.[66] This gift is the
spontaneous exhortation, warning, consolation, challenge, comfort, or
instruction to an individual or the body. Prophecy is not a natural
insight or judgment but a supernatural gift. It does not appear that
prophesies were expressed in the first person as was the case in the
Old Testament.[67] Paul's grace gift was prophecy.[68] He had a vision and
was tireless in pursuing it, and when things were wrong, he worked to
set them right. Paul was clear that the gift of prophecy was to be
desired by the church.[69]

Note: Some interpret Paul's statement "when the perfect comes..." (1
Cor. 13:8–10) to mean that the gifts of prophecy, tongues, and
knowledge would cease at the end of the apostolic period or the
closing of the canon of Scripture. They believe that the proclamation of
truth was then provided by teachers who searched the Scriptures.[70]
Others interpret those words to mean that the gift of prophecy will no
longer be needed when Christ comes for believers.

A person with the gift of prophecy:[71]

- Proclaims biblical truth spontaneously by divine inspiration;
- Calls the church to good order and discipline (1 Cor. 14:40);
- Provides comfort, encouragement, and conviction (1 Cor. 14:3);
- Recognizes false teaching; and
- Gives warning and instruction as it relates to various situations.

Serving (*diakonian*) — the Spirit-directed power to be God's hands and mind to the body of Christ. The word is also translated as ministry and is where we get the word deacon. Most commentators describe the gift of service in broad, general terms. This gift usually involves the application of a skill such as electrical, carpentry, plumbing, or mechanical (using the hands) or counseling or bookkeeping (using the mind). Some believe that serving is the most prominent gift in the church today.[72]

A person with the gift of serving:[73]

- Observes needs in the areas of their gifting and quickly acts to meet that need
- Acts to meet the needs of individuals or the body as a whole
- Ministers with joy
- Is always available
- Often puts the needs of others before their own
- Encourages others to serve

Teaching (*Didasko*) — the Spirit-directed power to present God's truth to the body of Christ. Teachers instruct (edify) the body. [74]
One with the gift of teaching:[75]

- Cares deeply for biblical truth
- Engages in critical analysis and interpretation of biblical truth
- Discovers what the Word says, what it means, and how it is to be applied
- Organizes and presents biblical truth

- Devotes himself to providing truth to others
- Focuses on biblical truth as opposed to other topics
- Delights in the opportunity to instruct others in teaching biblical truth
- Enjoys seeing lives transformed

Exhorting/Encouraging/Admonishing (*parakalon*) — the Spirit-directed persuasive power of God to inspire change in the lives of other believers. Encouragement motivates believers to seek a deeper walk with God (alter thinking or behavior). This gift is personal in nature. While teaching is aimed at the mind, encouragement is aimed at the heart. Prophecy, on the other hand, is aimed at the church, while encouragement is aimed at the individual. [76]

A person with the gift of encouragement:[77]

- Strengthens others through comfort, advice, reassurance, or warning
- Appeals to believers to live in obedience
- Persuades others with love, understanding, and sympathy

Contributing/Giving (*metadidous*) — the Spirit-directed allocation of one's God-given resources to meet the needs of others. Like the gift of service, the gift of giving does not necessarily require words or speaking.[78]

A person with the gift of giving:[79]

- Dispenses financial or material possessions to meet the needs of individuals or the body without encouragement or exhortation;
- Recognizes the needs of others
- Acknowledges that everything comes from God
- Communicates the love of God in tangible ways
- Sacrifices with joy the blessings God has provided
- Encourages others to participate in meeting a need

Leading/Ruling (*proistemenos*) — the Spirit-directed ability to identify and direct God's plans for advancing his kingdom within the local body or the body at large. The Greek communicates the idea of organizing, governing, administering, and ruling. One with this gift assists the pastor in overseeing ministries. (This is not the same as the overseer or bishop [*Episkopos*] as Paul discussed in 1 Timothy). This leading is distinct from secular leadership which is motivated by power and position and thus pursues secular methods and concepts.[80]

A person with the gift of leadership:[81]

- Envisions, organizes, plans, communicates, and administers a ministry or ministries
- Brings good order and discipline to the operation of the church
- Models behavior; sets an example
- Seeks the spiritual development of individuals and the church;
- Directs activities and functions with love, compassion, and concern for people and the body without coercion;
- Moves with eagerness and diligence to satisfy a need or needs within the body
- Engages others in carrying out a ministry or activity
- Knows the times in which one lives
- Is encouraged by seeing lives changed

Mercy (*eleeon*) — the Spirit-directed outpouring of the kindness, love, and compassion of God. This gift is provided without expecting anything in return. Mercy is action motivated by an observed need. It is a response to suffering. A person with this gift is motivated to meet one or several needs such as money, food, clothing, assistance with illness or the challenges of old age, depression, or other misfortunes. While the gift of service is applying skills in ministering to others, the gift of mercy is ministry from the heart.[82]

A person with the gift of mercy:[83]

- Recognizes needs and responds quickly and willingly
- Provides service cheerfully and with compassion

- Provides relief, comfort, and gentle words as needed
- May enlist others in meeting needs

Applying the Gift

To identify our grace gift, we must put ourselves in a position where the Holy Spirit can work. For example, a person may have the gift of encouragement but may not have a clue how it works. However, they can observe how people respond to them and receive feedback from those around them.

The following illustration shows how the different gifts can be applied in a hospital situation where a person is visited by people with different grace gifts.

- Mercy — "My heart goes out to you."
- Leadership — "Two others are keeping up your job while you're here."
- Giving — "How are you going to pay your bill? We can help."
- Encouragement/Exhortation—"This will help you grow in your faith."
- Teaching — "This is what the Word says about suffering."
- Serving — "Here, let me adjust the bed," and "Can I refill your water?"
- Prophecy — "Are you right with the Lord? Are there any sins you need to confess?"

While one's grace gift or focus is strongly indicated in a specific direction or application, it does not exempt us from ministering in other areas. Furthermore, a grace gift can manifest in different ways.

For example, a person with the gift of leadership can contribute in one or more of the following areas:

- Prophesying — expressing the vision
- Serving — participating in or leading activities that lend to a central goal, objective, or task

112

- Teaching — organization of materials for effective presentation
- Encouraging — warning if we do not stay the course
- Giving — devoting time, talent, and treasure to see the goal reached
- Mercy — willingness to help others

The Purpose of the Gift

Each member of the body is given a grace gift so that by its application, the body is made complete and operates effectively and efficiently. As members of the body, we must function according to the gifts we have been given. At the same time, there is to be unity within the diversity of gifts. Grace gifts are not for the individual but for the benefit of others or the body as a whole. We are called to serve others through our gift.

Varieties of Gifts	Varieties of Service (Needs)	Varieties of Workings (Results)
God	Lord	God
Gives the **Gift**	Directs **Service** to Needs	**Works** to Bring
▽	▽	▽
Believer ➡	Acts ➡	Results
Prophesy	Truth	Insight
Serving	Unmet needs	Needs met
Teaching	Lack of understanding	Application of the Word
Encouragement	Doubt/uncertainty	Confidence
Giving	Need/Deficit	Need met
Leadership	Lack of Direction	Guidance/Direction
Mercy	Need	Compassion

Figure 4. Grace Gifts in Action

What do people tell you is your grace gift? Where are you motivated to serve the Lord?

Christ in me: the motivation to serve.

SITUATION OR RESULTS GIFTS

Scripture

> To each is given the manifestation of the Spirit for the
> common good. For to one is given through the Spirit
> the utterance of wisdom, and to another the utterance
> of knowledge according to the same Spirit, to another
> faith by the same Spirit, to another gifts of healing by
> the one Spirit, to another the working of miracles, to
> another prophecy, to another the ability to distinguish
> between spirits, to another various kinds of tongues, to
> another the interpretation of tongues. All these are
> empowered by one and the same Spirit, who
> apportions to each one individually as he wills (1 Cor.
> 12:7–11).

Definition

While a grace gift is what a person does to build up the body,
situation or results gifts are the workings by the Spirit in an individual to
meet specific needs in others or the body. They are given by the Spirit
when needed and in the quantity needed.

The Context of the Passage

1 Corinthians: In this letter, Paul clarified the nature of salvation
through Christ and the need for love without discrimination. In
addition, he addressed the Corinthians' disorderly and self-centered
worship and the fact that they allowed immorality in their midst. Paul
also responded to requests for advice on several subjects and gave
instructions on correcting erroneous practices and false teachings,
among other things.[84]

1 Corinthians 12: During a dissertation on public worship begun in
chapter 11, Paul expressed concern about the Corinthian church's

knowledge of spiritual gifts and their misuse or abuse of gifts during worship. He began by dealing with situation gifts–gifts provided to meet specific needs in the body. As with his discussion on the grace gifts in Romans, Paul stressed the importance of unity among believers as members of one body. In this chapter, he used the human body to illustrate the proper functioning of the church. In so doing, he exhorted the church to bring balance to their view of spiritual gifts. Paul concluded the chapter by listing five additional gifts, which we will cover on pages 135–137.

The Giver of the Gifts

Paul states that: "All these [gifts] are empowered by one and the same Spirit, who apportions to each one individually as he wills." The Holy Spirit is the giver of situation gifts (1 Cor. 12:11).

The Nature of the Gifts

<u>Temporary</u>. While grace gifts are a permanent endowment in a believer, situational gifts are a temporary work of the Spirit through a believer to meet a specific need at a specific time. The verb form for "give" in the Greek (*didomi*) in verses seven and eight indicates that the gifts do not reside permanently in

> **Situation Gifts**
> - Utterance of Wisdom
> - Utterance of Knowledge
> - Faith
> - Healings
> - Working of Miracles
> - Prophesy
> - Distinguishing between Spirits
> - Various Tongues
> - The Interpretation of Tongues

believers. Nor are they permanently present in the body.[85]

<u>Need-based</u>. These gifts are given by the Spirit to believers as needed by the body. The gift is not given based on faith as with grace gifts but by the sovereign choice of the Spirit. He may equip one member of the body for a particular need and the next time use someone else for the same or different need.

<u>Gifts, Service, Workings</u>. As discussed in the introduction (page 109), Paul laid a foundation for this list of gifts:

> "Now there are varieties of gifts, but the same Spirit; and there are varieties of service, but the same Lord; and there are varieties of activities, but it is the same God who empowers them all in everyone" (1 Cor. 12:4–6).

- Gifts: a diversity provided, given, distributed, or allotted by the Spirit to believers
- Service: numerous ways of use as directed by the Lord
- Workings: multiple results brought about by God

Situational or results gifts are gifts of the Spirit working through believers to be used (as directed by Jesus) so that God can change lives.[86]

<u>Openness</u>. For God to produce results, the believer must be open or available to the working of the Spirit. At the same time, for results to be carried out, the intended person or group must be open to receiving the message or action. When a believer becomes aware that the Holy Spirit is inspiring them, they are to share it.

Note: Some speculate that in our rational, Western culture, we are not as open to these gifts as believers in other cultures who come out of a background of spiritism.

Are the gifts for today? In a related matter, some believe that many, if not all, of the gifts listed here ceased with the closing of the canon of Scripture based on their interpretation of 1 Corinthians 13:8–10.

> "Love never ends. As for prophecies, they will pass away; as for tongues, they will cease; as for knowledge, it will pass away. For we know in part and we prophesy in part, but when the perfect comes, the partial will pass away" (1 Cor. 13:8–10).

Others believe that Paul was referring to the perfection that comes when Christ returns for this church. Note that the arguments on both sides are compelling but scripture is not explicit on either interpretation. As theology professor Millard Erickson points out, God is sovereign and distributes gifts as he wills, and when he wills.[87]

Fairness. I have tried to be objective in describing situational gifts. However, it is important for you, the reader, to understand the lens through which I view the gifts. First, God desires that all come to a saving knowledge of him (1 Tim. 2:4) and grow to spiritual maturity (Heb. 6:1). Second, God is able and can do anything to advance his kingdom (Jer. 32:17; Matt. 26:19). Third, I came to understand my spiritual gifts because of engaging in ministry, not because I asked for them. Fourth, I believe that God, in his sovereignty, can and will bestow on me and others whatever gift he needs to advance his kingdom.

The Gifts

The utterance of wisdom (*sophias*) — the Spirit-motivated and inspired ability to declare an insight from God. Words of wisdom are not the expression of the wisdom of the world, ideas that come with maturity, or merely wise thinking. Wisdom is the ability to communicate guidance in specific situations consistent with Scripture. The message of wisdom focuses on the well-being of others or the body as a whole.[88]

Example: A church included a time of sharing during morning worship services. On several Sundays, a woman, new to the fellowship and without insight into the operation of the church, stood and urged the congregation to engage in personal and corporate outreach. It was something the church was neglecting.

Example: Pastor Eugene Givens had a vision in which he saw a dark SUV driving very slowly at night. He told his daughter-in-law about the vision and warned them to use extra caution on their trip home. That night, his son called to report that they had made it home but that there was an incident: A vehicle entered the highway on the right at high speed, forcing him to move into the left lane behind a slow-moving dark SUV. Due to the warning, they were prepared and able to avoid a collision.[89]

The utterance of knowledge (*gnoseos*) — the Spirit-motivated and inspired ability to receive, understand, and communicate truths about salvation, spiritual transformation, and their application to specific situations. It is in sharp contrast to worldly thoughts or philosophical ideas. It is a word that comes from the indwelling Spirit and not the knowledge of the individual. It is the ability to accurately express God-given supernatural, mystical, or profound insights. The message of knowledge is always consistent with Scripture.[90]

Example: A pastor's wife saw a man in the church one Sunday and immediately thought, "He is having an affair with his secretary." She relayed that insight to her husband. Three months later, the man and his wife came to the pastor, and before they could say anything, he told them that the man was having an affair and suggested they talk and pray about it. The couple were shocked that he knew about it.[91]

Example of two situational gifts: Givens and his wife were ministering in a church when the Spirit revealed to him that there was a deaf person in the congregation. A lady came forward with an infant who was deaf and shared that the baby was to have surgery the next day to correct the problem. Both he and his wife prayed that the Lord would give them the name of the doctor who would perform the surgery. The Spirit revealed that name to both independently. From that revelation, Givens believed that the Lord would heal the child (faith). The Lord healed the baby's hearing![92]

Faith (*pistis*) — the Spirit working through a believer to bring extraordinary conviction that God will move in a specific way or in a specific, impossible situation. It is not saving faith that all believers possess. Nor is it optimism, positive thinking, or naïve trust. It is pressing on during a hardship, trial, persecution, or martyrdom. It is a profound grasp of God's sovereign power and believing that he can overcome in life events in a most remarkable way. It is the ability to see beyond the immediate situation with an assurance that God will resolve the issue.[93]

Example: A believing friend confessed to having been in bondage to pornography for more than thirty years. I knew that God could deliver him. We dealt with the issues of commitment, surrender, and submission for several years until he committed his life to Christ. With that prayer, he was freed.

Example of three situational gifts: In a meeting in Denver, Givens was informed that someone had pain in both ankles. When he mentioned this to the fellowship (utterance of knowledge), a woman came forward, and Givens prayed for the Lord to heal that pain. He was then told that the woman was blind. Givens then prayed for her sight to be restored. While she was not healed that night, her daughter called the next morning exclaiming that her mother could see but was seeing double. Stepping out in faith that the Lord would completely restore her sight, Givens went to her and prayed for healing in Jesus's name. The woman's sight was fully restored (healing).[94]

Healing(s) (*iamaton*) — the Spirit working through a believer to restore health in a specific situation. Being in the plural, it indicates the ability to address a variety of ailments or needs. It would appear that Paul did not mean the natural ability of the body to restore health or through medicine or other medical actions, although the Lord does work in these ways. Nor does the language imply one healer for all situations. It includes sudden, gradual, physical, and mental healing.[95]

Example: A man was experiencing severe back pain. He had broken a leg in an accident years earlier, and when the leg healed, it was shorter than the other. Even with a built-up shoe, his back was stressed. He asked for prayer for his back in a men's group. One of the men said he would pray for the leg and not the back. The man's leg was healed! Example of two situational gifts: During a meeting, the Lord revealed to Givens that he was in the process of healing someone in the assembly. When Givens mentioned this to the fellowship (utterance of knowledge), a woman, who had a severe ankle injury stood and began walking without pain or the aid of the crutches with which she had come.[96]

Working of miracles (*energrmsts dynameon*) — the Spirit working through a believer in a specific situation to drive out demons (exorcism), gives judgment on unfaithful believers, or raise the dead. These are supernatural actions (actions that lie outside the normally understood and accepted laws of nature). Miracles are intended to bring clarity to the love and glory of God. They direct attention to the extraordinary power of God, meet human needs, and strengthen faith. They are carried out among believers.[97] They are an authentication of the gospel message.[98]

Example: The head of a Bible school was led by the Spirit to collect Bibles and transport them into a neighboring creative access country. They loaded the Bibles into a van and set off to the country on back roads without any more information than that. It was raining, and the road was muddy. In a remote area, the van slid off the road. As they prayed for help and guidance, a man knocked on the window. He asked them, "Did you bring the books?" He explained that he had had a vision of a man in white who told him that people would bring books to his village that would lead them to truth. He reported that he had been waiting by the road for three days.[99]

Example of two situational gifts: The Spirit revealed to Givens' wife that there was a woman present in a meeting who had extreme pain in her left hip and that she had difficulty standing up and sitting down. The Spirit revealed to Givens that the pain was caused by her left leg being shorter than the right. When Givens announced this to the congregation (utterance of knowledge), a woman came forward reporting that doctors had diagnosed the cause of her pain as a slipped disk in her back. Givens then informed the congregation that the Lord was going to grow her left leg (faith). He then, in the name of Jesus, commanded the leg to grow. The Lord restored the leg, and the pain was gone.[100]

Prophecy (*propheteia*) — definition of prophecy on page 115. Here, the Spirit works through a believer to address a specific need or situation. Prophecy is not permanent or ongoing in the individual as is the grace gift.

Example: One Sunday, Pastor John Piper was encouraging the people of Bethlehem Baptist Church to be involved in small groups and start evangelistic Bible studies. He said, "You might be working on the 34th floor of the IDS Tower, and maybe you should call your people together to have a small group meeting." After the service, a woman who had been sitting in the area where he had looked came up to him and said, "Why did you say that? I work on the 34th floor of the IDS Tower, and I've been praying about whether to start a small group."[101]

The ability to distinguish between spirits (*diakriseis pneumaton*) — the Spirit working through a believer to distinguish between true and false prophecy in a specific prophetic situation.[102]

Note: Some go beyond the assessment of prophecy, indicating the ability to discern evil spirits in a person or situation. Bible commentators Ciampa and Rosner limit the gift to the evaluation of prophecy because Paul listed it directly after prophecy.[103]

Example: While vacationing on the Olympic Peninsula, we walked through the city of Port Townsend. We entered a gift shop to buy postcards. We sensed an unmistakably heavy oppression. It was clearly satanic. We left immediately.

Example: Givens was asked to meet a man who had fallen on difficult times. He found the man and took him out to eat. During the meal, the man gazed at Givens with piercing eyes and spoke in an unnatural voice, saying, "I am the way" and "But your heart, Doc- tor Givens." He knew Givens was a doctor and had a previous heart condition. Givens recognized that the man was demon-possessed. Givens said, "I began to speak with great force, a litany of scriptures while staring straight into his eyes. 'No Satan, you are a liar. I belong to the most-high God . . . At the Name of Jesus, every knee will bow, now you bow your knee to the Name of Jesus and shut up.'" The man was humbled and stopped talking.[104]

Various kinds of tongues (*glosson*) — the Spirit working through a believer in a language that neither the speaker nor assembly knows or understands. Speaking in tongues is the working of the spirit for a specific time or situation. Paul allowed the use of tongues during public worship if there was an interpretation. That is, tongues must edify (1 Cor. 14:6–25). Paul stated that tongues are a sign to non-believers, quoting Isaiah 28:11–12. Also, it is important to remember that the Greek word "for to one is given..." (*didomi*), indicates that these gifts are temporary.[105]

Note: Paul allows for ecstatic utterances without interpretation but not in public worship. This would be what some call a private prayer language or praying in the Spirit (1 Cor. 14:13–19). That is not the gift that Paul addresses here in verses ten and twenty-eight.[106]

Example: Rev. Ruolneihum (kuh-ma) Pakhuongte was sharing the gospel to a small, unevangelized village in Assam province, India. The people of the village spoke a language he did not know, and no interpreter was available. He was led by the Spirit to preach to them in his own language. At the end of the message, he gave an invitation for salvation, and the entire village responded. They had heard the message in their own language. Kuhma said he had never experienced this before or since.[107]

Interpretation of tongues (*hermeniea*) — the Spirit-motivated and inspired ability to bring understanding to what has just been said in tongues in the assembly by someone other than the speaker in tongues.[108]

The Purpose of the Gifts

The purpose of situational or results gifts is to transform individuals or a group to whom the Lord wants to minister. These gifts are not for the believer through whom the Spirit works. God then uses those words or actions to bring clarity of thought, insight, consolation, encouragement, or restoration to an individual or the body as a whole. As Paul put it, the gifts are intended for the common good (v. 7). When a gift is applied, there is an awareness on the part of the person through whom the Spirit works that God is at work and what is happening needs to be shared with an individual or group. On the part of the person or group receiving the message or action, there is an awareness that the Lord is working supernaturally to bring about transformation, restoration, or other results.

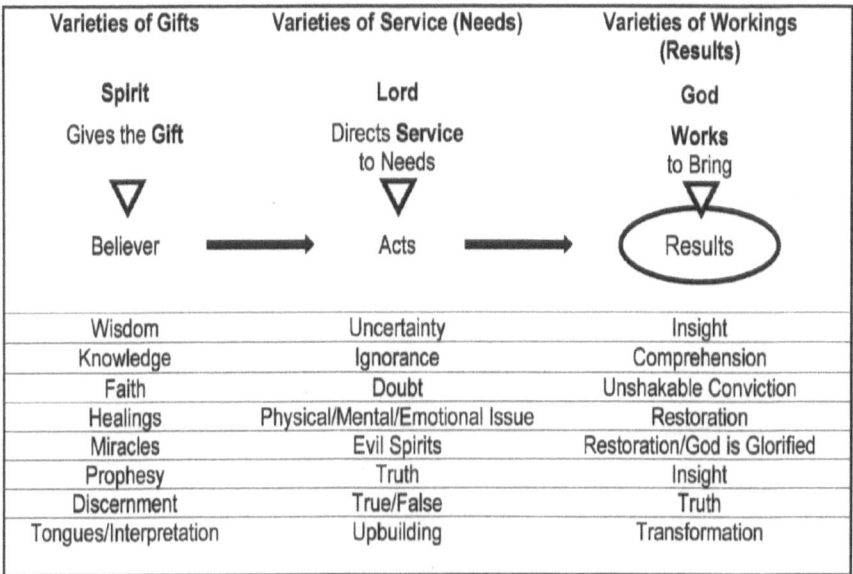

Varieties of Gifts	Varieties of Service (Needs)	Varieties of Workings (Results)
Spirit	**Lord**	**God**
Gives the **Gift**	Directs **Service** to Needs	**Works** to Bring
▽	▽	▽
Believer ⟶	Acts ⟶	Results
Wisdom	Uncertainty	Insight
Knowledge	Ignorance	Comprehension
Faith	Doubt	Unshakable Conviction
Healings	Physical/Mental/Emotional Issue	Restoration
Miracles	Evil Spirits	Restoration/God is Glorified
Prophesy	Truth	Insight
Discernment	True/False	Truth
Tongues/Interpretation	Upbuilding	Transformation

Figure 5. Situation Gifts in Action

Where have you experienced the Spirit working through you to impact the lives of others?

Christ in me: the Spirit responding to a need.

BODY GIFTS

Scripture

Now you are the body of Christ and individually members of it. And God has appointed in the church first apostles, second prophets, third teachers, then miracles, then gifts of healing, helping, administrating, and various kinds of tongues. Are all apostles? Are all prophets? Are all teachers? Do all work miracles? Do all possess gifts of healing? Do all speak with tongues? Do all interpret? But earnestly desire the higher gifts. And I will show you a still more excellent way (1 Cor. 12:27–31).

Definition

God's plan is for members of the body of Christ to receive spiritual blessings from each other for building up the body.

Context of the Passage

See context for situation or results gifts on page 122.

Giver of the Gifts

God is the giver of body gifts ("God has appointed..." 1 Cor. 12:28).

The Nature of the Gifts

The gifts listed in verse twenty-eight follow Paul's essay on the importance of unity within the church given the variety of gifts. He used the human body as an example: all parts (gifts) working together for efficient and effective operation (of the church). From this, we classify these spiritual gifts as body gifts. Commentators Morris and Adkins believe that God appointed, dispensed, or set in place, these nine gifts in the church universal.[109] As such, they are permanent in the church but only applied through individuals temporarily as determined by God. The first three roles: apostles, prophets, and teachers are well-defined leadership positions or roles.[110] Paul numbers them to indicate the sequence in the development of the church: apostles plant, prophets establish truth, and teachers edify.[111] The remaining six gifts are dispensed to the church as and where needed. Four of the six are repeated from the situational gifts in verses eight through ten, leading some to define them as situational gifts.[112] Together, these gifts work to bring unity and efficiency to the operation of the church.

Leadership Appointments (People)

Apostles (*apostolous*) — ones sent with authority; those commissioned by Christ in a resurrection appearance and sent out to establish the church (church planters). They were accountable to Christ and spoke with his authority. They were foundational to the church and, like Paul, itinerant. Apostleship was a role, not an office or position in the early church.[113]

An apostle:[114]

- Spoke with the authority of God
- Planted churches
- Equipped with many gifts
- Prepared those who would carry on the ministry in the local church
- Equipped the body for the work of ministry
- Was itinerant—moved about as the Spirit directed
- Reported back to the sending church

Note: Many believe that the term applies to the original eleven plus Paul and that the role is not present in the church today. Some understand Luke and Paul to have used the term in an informal sense when referring to Andronicus, Junias, Barnabas, James, Silas, and Timothy.[115]

Prophets (*prophetas*) — believers with the gift of prophecy. See the grace gift of prophecy, page 115. They spoke in the local body, most likely during worship (1 Cor. 14:36–39). They were foundational in leading and developing the early church.[116]

Note: Because prophets were essential for planting the early church, many today believe that this role ceased with the closing of the canon of Scripture.[117] On the other hand, others believe that prophecy continues today through believers motivated and inspired by the Spirit in a given situation but not necessarily vested in one individual as defined above.[118]

Teachers (*didaskalous*) — believers with the gift of teaching. See the grace gift of teaching, page 116. Teachers were empowered to pass on the theological traditions established[119] by the apostles. In the early church, they were foundational in setting aside the rabbinic traditions and interpretations brought forward by Jewish believers. They were essential in an age when copies of texts were not available.[120]

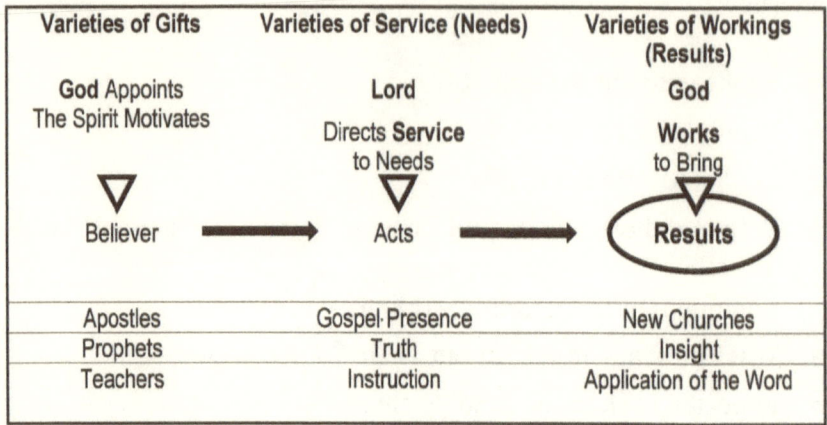

Varieties of Gifts	Varieties of Service (Needs)	Varieties of Workings (Results)
God Appoints The Spirit Motivates	**Lord** Directs **Service** to Needs	**God** **Works** to Bring
Believer ➡	Acts ➡	**Results**
Apostles	Gospel·Presence	New Churches
Prophets	Truth	Insight
Teachers	Instruction	Application of the Word

Figure 6. Leadership Roles

Situational Gifts

Paul continued the list of bodily gifts by repeating four situational gifts and adding two. He repeated what can be called "spectaculars gifts:" miracles, healings, tongues, and interpretation. To those he added helping and administrating, suggesting that other workings of the Spirit were equally important. Again, believers are the conduit through which the Spirit works as needed by God.

Miracles (*dynameis*) — the Spirit working through believers to produce miracles. See the situational gift of the working of miracles on page 128. Paul set miracles apart from the three leadership gifts by the word "then" (*epeita*), indicating he had moved on from endowment gifts. However, some believe that because this gift is not preceded by "gifts of...," they are a fourth group in the church but of lesser importance than apostles, prophets, and teachers. Bible scholar and translator D. K. Lowery believes that apostles, prophets, and teachers ministered to the whole church and that Paul's focus for the rest of the list was addressed to the Corinthian church and local churches.[121]

<u>Healing</u> (*iamaton*) — the Spirit working through believers to restore physical, mental, and spiritual health. Healing is a gift given permanently to the church but exercised by people of humility and faith as the situation dictates.[122] See the situational gift of healings on page 127.

<u>Helping</u> (*antilempseis*) — the Spirit working through believers to provide practical assistance to others, principally the poor and sick or those socially disadvantaged in the body of Christ. This word is only used here in the New Testament but numerous times in the Greek Old Testament; those with the gift of helping take on a load from those heavily burdened.[123] This ministry may or may not be carried out by those with the grace gift of service. By using a different word from the grace gift of service (diakonian), Paul may be making the distinction between the endowment and this situational gift.

Example: After Hurricane Katrina, a man from southern Alabama went to Waveland, Mississippi, set up a kitchen, and began cooking for relief workers and those in need. He continued doing so until Samaritans Purse and federal relief agencies were in place and operating.

<u>Administrating</u> (*kyberneseis*) — the Spirit working through believers to develop strategies, organize resources, and provide sound advice and guidance on the operation of a ministry or church; a helmsman who guides or directs the church on its God-given course; one who governs. This word is only used here in the New Testament.[124] The word is in the plural, which may mean there were more than one person used in the church or multiple functions associated with the working of the Spirit. The distinction between administrating and the grace gift of leadership or ruling (*proistemi*) is not clear. Administrating may provide support to one who rules or leads. This ministry may or may not always be carried out by those with the grace gift of leadership. By using a different word from the grace gift of leadership (*proistemenos*), Paul may be making the distinction between the endowment and this situational gift.

Example: A new member of a congregation noticed that proper accounting procedures were not being followed and took action to make improvements.

Various kinds of tongues (*glosson*) — See the situational gift of tongues on page 130. It should be noted that the gift of tongues is listed last both here and in verse ten because the Corinthian church considered it to be of greater prominence than was appropriate.[125]

Interpretation (*diermeneosin*) — Mentioned in verse thirty-one. See situational gifts on page 130. The word Paul used here is a strengthened form of *hermeniea* used in verse ten. It means to translate or make understandable primarily to outsiders or non-Jews.[126] Paul went on in chapter fourteen to say that interpretation is essential to validate tongues during public worship. Obviously, Paul did two things here: he again put tongues and interpretation at the bottom of the list and specified the purpose of the gifts.

Purpose of the Gifts

Bodily gifts are given or set into the church for the common good. They are the Spirit at work to build up individuals and the church locally, regionally, and globally.

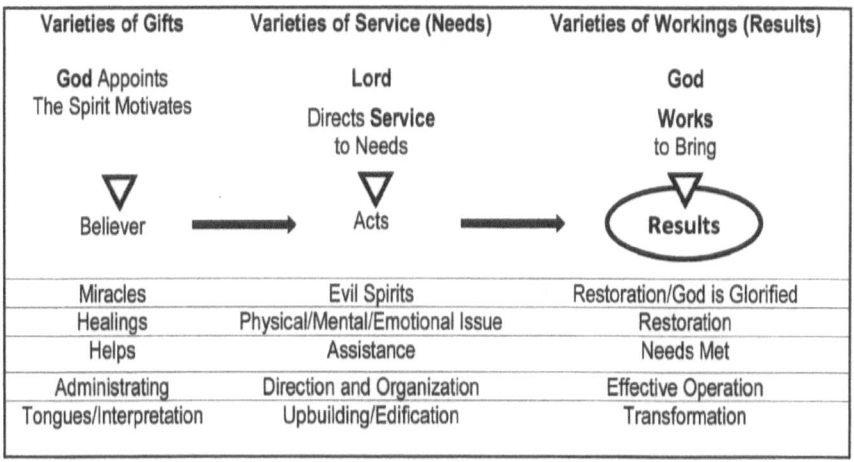

Varieties of Gifts	Varieties of Service (Needs)	Varieties of Workings (Results)
God Appoints The Spirit Motivates	**Lord** Directs **Service** to Needs	**God** **Works** to Bring
▽ Believer ➡	▽ Acts ➡	▽ (Results)
Miracles	Evil Spirits	Restoration/God is Glorified
Healings	Physical/Mental/Emotional Issue	Restoration
Helps	Assistance	Needs Met
Administrating	Direction and Organization	Effective Operation
Tongues/Interpretation	Upbuilding/Edification	Transformation

Figure 7. Body Gifts in Action

Diversity, Desire, and Devotion

Paul continued his discussion of bodily gifts by making three points:

First, just as the human body consists of different but interdependent parts, so the church consists of believers with different gifts. But all the gifts are needed for the effective operation of the body. The gifts are distributed across the body by God for the common good. None of the gifts are any more important than any other, nor are any gifts seen as more or less evidence of one's spirituality.[127]

Second, Paul urged the Corinthians to seek more ordinary gifts such as prophecy rather than the more dramatic gifts of miracles and tongues. That is, the church needed to desire the gifts that were most beneficial to the body. Tongues are not beneficial unless there is interpretation. The Corinthians needed to seek interpretation of tongues. Paul's major point, however, is that spiritual gifts should be exercised in love.[128]

Third, while the gifts are an excellent way of ministering to one another and the body, Paul told the Corinthians, and us today, that there is a "more excellent way" of living. He continued his letter by exhorting the church to live out the fruit of the Spirit, chief among them being love. Paul called the church to a life in Christ. Christ demonstrated love through his death, burial, and resurrection. Paul urged the church to minister in love, the more excellent way.[129]

Where has God appointed you? Where has the Spirit worked through you to build up the body?

Christ in me: building up the body.

LEADERSHIP GIFTS

Scripture

> And he gave the apostles, the prophets, the evangelists, the shepherds and teachers, to equip the saints for the work of ministry, for building up the body of Christ, until we all attain to the unity of the faith and of the knowledge of the Son of God, to mature manhood, to the measure of the stature of the fullness of Christ, so that we may no longer be children, tossed to and fro by the waves and carried about by every wind of doctrine, by human cunning, by craftiness in deceitful schemes. Rather, speaking the truth in love, we are to grow up in every way into him who is the head, into Christ, from whom the whole body, joined and held together by every joint with which it is equipped, when each part is working properly, makes the body grow so that it builds itself up in love (Eph. 4:11–16).

Definition

Leadership gifts are given to the church by Jesus to equip believers for works of service (discipling or building up the body).

Context of the Passage

Ephesians: The purpose of the letter to the Ephesians was to expand the vision of the church to the dimensions of God's eternal purpose and grace and encourage the church to appreciate the high calling God has for the body.

Ephesians 4: Paul concluded chapter three with a prayer for the Ephesians. He changed the focus in chapter four to the unity of the body of Christ. As in Romans 12 and 1 Corinthians 12, he stressed that the church is one body under Christ, and as such, Christ dispenses gifts of leadership to prepare believers for works of service, the building up of the body, motivating it toward maturity and attaining the whole measure of the fullness of Christ. He concluded chapter four by defining what it means to be a mature believer.

The Nature of the Gifts

Leadership gifts are given to Spirit-directed and inspired believers for advancing Christ's kingdom locally, regionally, or globally. The gifts are given according to the measure or standard of Christ. The gift is freely given, at the will of Jesus, as he sees fit and without condition. Leadership gifts represent a calling to a ministry that is permanent and foundational. If a person does not respond to the call, a blessing is lost to both the individual and the body. If a person rejects the calling, another will be called, illustrating the distinction between God's perfect will and God's permissive will.

Giver of the Gifts

Jesus is the giver of leadership gifts. Preceding the above verses, Paul stated, in verse 4:8, that he, Jesus, ascended and descended. He then said: "And he himself [Jesus] gave some to be..." (Eph. 4:11). Jesus earned the right to give these gifts through his death, burial, and resurrection. "He is the head of the body, the church. He is the beginning, the firstborn from the dead, that in everything he might be preeminent" (Col. 1:18). In giving these gifts, Jesus is being obedient to the Father who ordained these requirements.

The Gifts

Apostles (*Apostolious*) — see body gift of apostle on page 133.

Prophets (*prophetas*) — see the grace gift of prophecy on page 115. It must be noted that prophet or prophecy is listed on all four lists indicating the importance Paul gave in proclaiming truth.

Evangelist (*evangelistes*) — (1) a believer motivated and inspired by the Spirit to proclaim the gospel; one who brings others into the body of Christ as opposed to apostles and prophets who edify and build up the body; an activity rather than an office; usually itinerant; a missionary. (2) A believer gifted in leading others to Christ.[130] An evangelist:[131]

- Itinerant, considered to be missionaries
- Proclaims the good news
- Leads people to Christ
- Builds up new believers
- Gives testimony to what God has done in their lives
- Seeks converts
- Assists apostles in building the church

Shepherd and Teacher (*poimen kai didaskalos*) — a believer gifted by the Spirit to lead a local church through comfort, guidance, encouragement, care, and instruction (the Greek does not have an article before teacher and the conjunction *kai* Paul uses, indicating that Paul saw these responsibilities as resident in one person); a person responsible for building up the body in the faith and in numbers; a function rather than an office since the Greek word for office is not used in the New Testament. Commentator John Stott indicates that Paul began using the terms "presbyter, bishop, and overseer for leaders of the church later in the pastoral epistles."[132]

A shepherd/teacher:[133]

- Provides comfort, nurture, and guidance to the local body
- Provides instruction to the body (feeds the flock)
- Protects the body from spiritual danger
- Oversees the day-to-day operation of a church
- Calls and prepares others to minister
- Leads the local body

The Purpose of the Gifts

Leadership gifts are given to the church to mend, restore, prepare, or complete believers who, in turn, perform works of service that bring about unity in the faith, knowledge of the Son of God, steadfast growth into the likeness of Christ, and the ability to withstand deceit and the craftiness of false doctrine. These gifts are given for the common good to train people in service to the Lord and lead them in advancing the kingdom. They are given to bind the body together. They are necessary and required for building up the church. The image is of a well-oiled machine directed by Christ (the head) effectively working through designated leaders.[134]

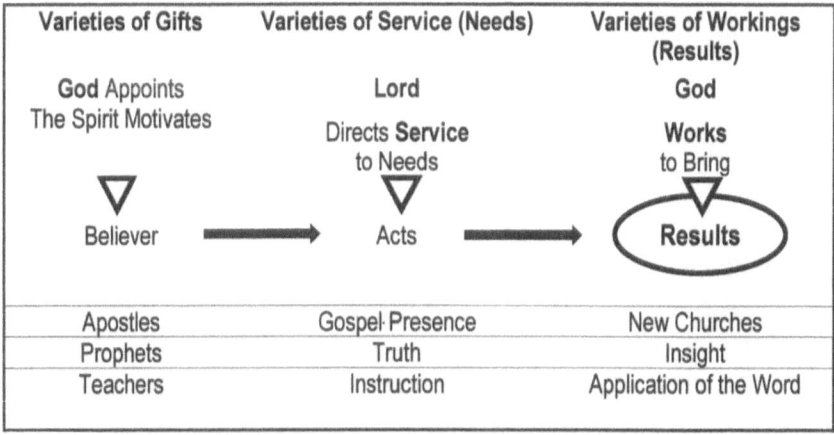

Figure 8. Leadership Gifts in Action

Are you a church planter or missionary? Do you provide comfort, encouragement, or conviction? Or are you an evangelist or a teacher?

Christ in me: leading the body of Christ.

CONCLUDING THOUGHTS ON SPIRITUAL GIFTS

God in Action

Recently, a friend I had not seen in some time said, "You changed my life!" He was referring to a neighborhood Bible study I led. While that encouraged me, he was not correct. All I did was apply my spiritual gift when and where the Lord directed it. It was God who changed his life. When believers use their spiritual gift as the Lord leads, God will bring about the results. This is an example of God being intimately involved in his creation. God has a plan and will not change it as he said in Isaiah:

> I am God, and there is none like me,
> declaring the end from the beginning
> and from ancient times things not yet done,
> saying, My counsel shall stand,
> and I will accomplish all my purpose,
> calling a bird of prey from the east,
> the man of my counsel from a far country.
> I have spoken, and I will bring it to pass;
> I have purposed, and I will do it (Isa. 46:9–11).

God has calls and equips us to be a part of his plan. He will carry out that plan through you or me, or he will find someone else to do it. He said it will happen. We are uniquely called and equipped to move, act, and communicate as the Spirit works in us as directed by the Lord so that God will bring results and glorify himself.

The Spirit in Me

I am constantly amazed that God will change the world through us feeble, frail, and fumbling human beings. At the same time, that thought motivates me to allow him to work through me in changing that part of the world he has defined for me. It is clear to me that I do not have the wisdom, strength, and determination to do what he expects. Fortunately, he has placed his Spirit in me to first transform my life so that, in some small way, I am Christ to my world. Second, he has gifted me to make a difference in the lives of others and churches in which God has placed me over the years. I am motivated to lead, teach, and administer. I have worked with several shepherds and teachers, helpers, encouragers, and evangelists. By working together, we see God changing lives and advancing his kingdom.

He changes lives and advances his kingdom but only through those who have unleashed the Spirit. Paul admonished the Thessalonian church not to quench the Spirit. He went on to warn the church not to "despise prophesies" (1 Thess. 5:19–20). Many conclude that he meant not to throw cold water on the fire of spiritual gifts.[135] Quenching the Spirit can mean the failure to exercise one's spiritual gift out of ignorance or fear.

In Romans 11:29, Paul said, "For the gifts and the calling of God are irrevocable." He provides spiritual gifts to believers to change the world. If we do not apply them, we lose the blessing, not the gift.

Unity in Diversity

Paul referred to the church as one body and individuals as members of that body. We all are to work together for a common purpose, building up the body. Unity in the church is often compared to an orchestra where different musicians play different notes on different instruments but together produce the sound that the composer intended. Another example is members of a construction crew employing different skills and tools in building a house as the architect intended. There is to be both unity and diversity in the body of Christ.

While this sounds reasonable, it is possible only when believers are

Spirit-led. Believers are equipped uniquely to work together to achieve God's plan. When that happens, the result is supernatural.

Clarity in Complexity

While there is duplication of gifts between the four types of gifts, it is important to recognize the differences between where and how the gifts are to be used.

- Grace gifts are given by God to complete the body. They are the building blocks of the church.
- Situational gifts are given by the Holy Spirit to different individuals at different times to meet a specific need. They are the energy of the church.
- Bodily gifts are given by God to build up individuals or the body. They bring results.
- Leadership gifts are given by Jesus to bring individuals and the church to spiritual maturity. They are the foundation of the church.

As mentioned earlier, some commentators suggest that the twenty gifts listed in four passages are only a partial list. I recall a previous study of the gifts that listed twenty-nine gifts. One could argue that some in that list are variations of the gifts Paul listed in his four letters.

Table 3. Spiritual Gifts Across Paul's Lists

	Gifts	Grace Rom. 12:6–8	Situational 1 Cor. 12:7–11	Bodily 1 Cor. 12:28–31	Leadership Eph. 4:11
1	Prophecy	•	•	•	•
2	Serving	•			
3	Teaching	•		.	
4	Exhorting/ Encouraging	•			
5	Contributing/ Giving	•			
6	Leading	•			
7	Mercy	•			
8	Wisdom		•		
9	Knowledge		•		
10	Faith		•		
11	Healing		•	•	
12	Miracles		•	•	
13	Discernment		•	•	
14	Tongues		•	•	
15	Interpretation		•	•	
16	Apostles			•	•
17	Helping			•	
18	Administrating			•	
19	Evangelist				•
20	Shepherd/ Teacher				•

Spiritual Gifts in Me (Finding My Spiritual Gift)

"The counsel of the Lord stands forever, the plans of his heart to all generations" (Ps. 33:11). What a privilege it is to carry out that plan. To do that, we must recognize and give the Spirit freedom to work in and through us. But how can we know what our gifts are and where do we apply them? The most important step in finding your spiritual gift is to engage in serving or ministering to others.

- What activities or ministries appeal to you?
- Where are you motivated to engage: with your mind, hands, or heart?
- When and where have you seen God work through you?
- What is your passion?
- Where do people ask you to serve?
- What gift or gifts do people say you have; what have they observed in the way you serve or where you serve?

Have you surrendered your life to the Lord and given the Spirit freedom to work through you? How has the Lord defined your "world?" Where is the Spirit working through you to advance the kingdom?

Table 4. Spiritual Gifts Summary

	Grace Gifts	Situational/ Results Gifts	Bodily Gifts	Leadership Gifts
Reference	Rom. 12:6–8	1 Cor. 12:7–11	1 Cor. 12:27–31	Eph. 4:10–16
Giver	God	Holy Spirit	God	Jesus
Gifts	•Prophesying •Serving •Teaching •Encouraging •Giving •Leadership •Mercy	•Wisdom •Knowledge •Faith •Healings •Miraculous Powers •Prophecy •Discernment •Tongues •Interpretation	•First apostles •Second prophets •Third teachers •Miracles •Healing •Helping •Administering •Tongues •Interpretation	•Apostle •Prophet •Evangelist •Shepherd/ Teacher
Context	•Live righteously •Apply doctrine of faith •Be living sacrifices •Be humble •Work together as part of one body	•Know when and where to use the gifts •Seek unity in diversity •Work as a part of one body •Exercise in love	•Know when and where to use the gifts •Seek unity in diversity •Work as a part of one body •Exercise in love	•Bring every believer to maturity in Christ
Nature	•Each has one gift •The motivating factor in one's life •Permanent •Shapes our view of ministry and people •One gift but may be manifest in many ways	•Temporary •Need-based •Spirit-given •Lord-directed •God brings results •Requires openness to working •Given to be shared	•Essential to the body •Permanent to the body •Leadership of the body •As needed by the body	•A calling •Required •Functions within the church •Given by Jesus based on the authority coming from his resurrection
Purpose	•Together with others; makes the body complete •For the benefit of others or the body •Edification of the body	•To meet individual needs •For the edification of the body •For the common good	•These are gifts given to build up individuals and, working together, build up the body	•Prepare believers to perform works of service •Bring unity of faith •Attain the complete measure of the fullness of Christ

Christ in me: God's hand in my glove.

Empowered DiscipleMaking

ADVANCING HIS KINGDOM

And Jesus came and said to them, "All authority in heaven and on earth has been given to me. Go therefore and make disciples of all nations, baptizing them in the name of the Father and of the Son and of the Holy Spirit, teaching them to observe all that I have commanded you. And behold, I am with you always, to the end of the age" (Matt. 28:18–20).

THE COMMAND

*J*esus's purpose in calling his disciples was for them to make disciples. He spent three years preparing his disciples for this task. His purpose in calling us is also to make disciples. His call to make disciples was repeated five times in the statements below (emphasis added).

"Follow me, and **I will make you fishers of men**" (Matt. 4:20).

"Go therefore and **make disciples of all nations...**" (Matt. 28:19).

"Go into all the world and **proclaim the gospel** to the whole creation" (Mark 16:15).

"As the Father has sent me, even so **I am sending you**"

(John 20:21).

"But you will receive power when the Holy Spirit has come upon you, and **you will be my witnesses** in Jerusalem and in all Judea and Samaria, and to the end of the earth" (Acts 1:8).

What does the Great Commission mean to you? Where has he called you to serve? Is it Jerusalem, Judea, Samaria, or the world? What has he called you to do?

Christ in me: advancing his kingdom whenever, wherever, and however he has called.

WHAT IS A DISCIPLE?

"Follow me and I will make you fishers of men" (Matt. 4:19).

Becoming a disciple is an intentional process. Discipleship leads to disciplemaking. We are called to bring new believers into the body of Christ, lead them to a deeper, dynamic relationship with the Lord, and send them out as disciplemakers.

What does it mean to be a Christian?

In our society, the term Christian has come to have a variety of meanings. For some, it means they are not Hindu, Buddhist, Muslim, atheist, and so on. There are cults who consider themselves to be Christian. An American asked an English friend if she was a Christian. The woman answered in amazement, "Of course, I'm English!" For some, it means attending or identifying with a church. For still others, it means living a good life, serving others, and giving to charity. It has been said that if you ask ten people to define what it means to be a Christian, you will get eight answers.

142

The word "Christian" is used three times in the New Testament. First, in Antioch (Acts 11:26), then at Paul's trial before Agrippa (Acts 26:28), and finally when Peter encouraged believers who were abused for their faith (1 Pet. 4:14–16). Clearly, New Testament Christians were set apart from the rest of society because of their beliefs, attitudes, and behavior. Being set apart means they had made a conscious decision to accept Christ as their personal Savior and had made him the Lord of their lives. However, in our society and even in our churches, those who call themselves Christian may not have taken the step of faith to salvation, are not aware of the new life salvation brings, or see no need to grow in their faith.

What is a disciple?

In response to this question, people often say, "Yes, I'm a follower of Jesus" without understanding the significance of the term. The term disciple has Old Testament roots. Some considered themselves to be disciples of Moses (John 9:28). John the Baptist had disciples. Jesus had many followers, people who believed in him as a real person with great power. Not all, however, were disciples. Jesus clarified the issue of discipleship in Luke.

> If anyone comes to me and does not hate his own father and mother and wife and children and brothers and sisters, yes, and even his own life, he cannot be my disciple. Whoever does not bear his own cross and come after me cannot be my disciple. For which of you, desiring to build a tower, does not first sit down and count the cost, whether he has enough to complete it? Otherwise, when he has laid a foundation and is not able to finish, all who see It begin to mock him, saying, "This man began to build and was not able to finish." Or what king, going out to encounter another king in war, will not sit down first and deliberate whether he is able with ten thousand to meet him who comes against him with twenty thousand? And if not, while the other is yet a great way off, he sends a delegation and asks for terms

of peace. So therefore, any one of you who does not renounce all that he has cannot be my disciple (Luke 14:26–33).

Kyle Idleman, in his book, *Not a Fan*, defines a follower of Jesus in terms of being committed to Christ, having an intimate relationship with him, a singular focus, and being spirit led.[136] Idleman goes on to state that a follower will go wherever and whenever and do whatever Jesus asks. He challenges his readers with Luke 9:23: "And he said to all, 'If anyone would come after me, let him deny himself and take up his cross daily and follow me.'" That means total commitment. A follower by this definition is a disciple.

Steve Murrell, pastor, church planter, and missionary states that:

A disciple is someone who follows Jesus, "fishes" for people and does this in fellowship with other disciples, while carrying a cross. Discipleship is not complicated. Difficult, yes. Complicated, no. It is so simple that a carpenter described it to uneducated fishermen 2,000 years ago in one sentence: "Follow me and I will make you fishers of men" (Matt. 4:19).[137]

God's Plan

God intends that when a person is saved, they should: (1) be taught the fundamentals of the faith, (2) be shown the biblical instruction for holy living and obedience, (3) be led to victories over the issues that interfere with discipleship, and (4) become disciplemakers. God's intention is for this process to be seamless, always moving us from where we are to where God wants us to be.

Discipleship involves putting aside one's personal agenda, defining the cost, and setting priorities. The most compelling command to his disciples was to go and make disciples (Matt. 28:18–20). In the book of Acts, we see men whose faith went beyond belief in Jesus for salvation. They moved out in faith and the power of the Holy Spirit. Discipleship means moving beyond passive acceptance of salvation, actively surrendering to the power of the Spirit, and being passionately engaged in serving the Lord.

"And a large crowd was following him, because they saw the signs that he was doing on the sick. When many of his disciples heard it, they said, "This is a hard saying; who can listen to it?"After this many of his disciples turned back and no longer walked with him" (John 6:2, 60, 66).

Scripture makes a clear distinction between crowds and disciples.

The Secret to Making Disciples

The secret is that we do not make disciples. That is the job of the Holy Spirit. The work of the Spirit is to "convict the world of sin, of righteousness, and of judgment" (John 16:8).

Dietrich Bonhoeffer says, "Christianity without discipleship is always Christianity without Christ."[138]

How do you define discipleship? Are you a disciple?

Christ in me: equipped to be a disciple.

REACHING THE LOST

The customary practice of Jesus's day was for men who wanted to go beyond the first two levels of Jewish schooling to select a rabbi to follow and then leave everything behind. They were called *Talmidim*. They spent the next fifteen years literally copying their rabbi in behavior and words and in the study of the Talmud.[139]

Jesus, on the other hand, called his disciples. He selected those he wanted to follow him. He picked men who likely had not gone beyond the first level of Jewish education, the synagogue school for boys and girls six to twelve years old.[140]

He told them he would make them "fishers of men." He described the outcome of following him in terms that fishermen understood. He did not tell them they were to become rabbis. Yet, the language he used in the Great Commission was exactly that: They were to make followers of Jesus.

Before going any further, we need to note that new believers in Jerusalem at Pentecost turned the world upside down without evangelism or discipleship training.

He Commissioned Them

> "And he called to him his twelve disciples and gave them authority over unclean spirits, to cast them out, and to heal every disease and every affliction" (Matt. 10:1).

There are eight references to Jesus's disciples prior to chapter 10. Matthew records his own calling in 8:9.[141] Therefore, Jesus had already called his disciples. So, in the verse above, he was commissioning his disciples.

Some consider Jesus to have selected his disciples from his followers. That may have been the case for Matthew, as Jesus always seemed to have either a crowd or his disciples following him. However, in the Mark and John accounts of their calling, Jesus was alone with them when he called them.

Why did Jesus select the men he did? First, he knew their hearts. He selected those he knew would advance his kingdom. Second, he selected ordinary men because they were similar to the people to whom he was ministering. Third, he selected them to demonstrate to the people of that day, and to us, that his message could be carried to the world by people who had limited formal education and were not highly regarded by society.

Are all followers or believers called to be disciples? The Lord issues the salvation call to everyone. Upon salvation, he places the Holy Spirit in us (Rom. 8:9–11) to advance his kingdom. Peter tells us we are a "royal priesthood" chosen to advance his kingdom (1 Pet. 2:9). Yes, all are called to be disciples.

He Gave Them Authority

"And he called to him his twelve disciples and **gave them authority** over unclean spirits, to cast them out, and to heal every disease and every affliction" (Matt. 10:1, emphasis added).

Jesus commissioned them to drive out unclean spirits and heal every affliction. Clearly, they had seen Jesus perform miracles. Now, he was telling them that they were to do the same. But note, he gave them authority (*exousia*) over the evil spirits and afflictions. Luke 9:1 says that Jesus empowered (*dynamis*) them.

From a purely human perspective, it is difficult to grasp that they, and we, can exercise supernatural powers. Yet, Mark's account reports that this is exactly what they did. As pointed out in the discussion of spiritual gifts, we have been given spiritual gifts that allow us to minister far beyond our human abilities.

He Organized Them

"The names of the twelve apostles are these: first, Simon, who is called Peter, and Andrew his brother; James the son of Zebedee, and John his brother; Philip and Bartholomew; Thomas and Matthew the tax collector; James the son of Alphaeus, and Thaddaeus; Simon the Cananaean, and Judas Iscariot, who betrayed him" (Matt. 10:2–4).

Jesus came to seek and save the lost (Luke 19:10). At another place, Jesus looked over a field and declared that it was ready for harvest (John 4:35). His plan is for all to come to a saving knowledge of Jesus Christ. But Jesus (God in human form) was limited by time and space. To reach people with the gospel after his earthly life was over, he formed a team to carry on his work.

Notice that the disciples are listed in pairs. In Mark 6:7 and Luke 10:1, Jesus sent his followers out two by two. In other words, we are not to minister alone. Each of us brings different insight into the situation.

Moreover, we need to reach the lost as a broader team. We are to pray for one another, encourage each other, and rejoice together in success. On the other hand, we see examples in Scripture of individuals leading people to the Lord; for example, Phillip and the Ethiopian eunuch and Paul and the centurion.

We are a team. We have been given different spiritual gifts so that together we can do what we cannot do alone. If we as individuals and as a body are not advancing Christ's kingdom, we are impeding it. Remember, there are different roles in advancing the kingdom: one plants, another waters, and yet a third may harvest. Some are prayer warriors, others build relationships, and still others present the gospel. Some of us can do all three.

He Told Them to Whom They Were to Go

> "These twelve Jesus sent out, instructing them, 'Go nowhere among the Gentiles and enter no town of the Samaritans, but go rather to the lost sheep of the house of Israel'" (Matt. 10:5–6).

These instructions are far different from "Go into all the world" as mentioned in Matthew 28:18–20 and Acts 1:8. While no explanation is given, there may be several reasons. First, Jesus's own focus was on his children, the Jews. Even Paul went to the Jews first. Second, the disciples' message was rooted in the Law and the Prophets, something the Jews understood. Third, the Jews were nearby and shared a similar culture. Fourth, the disciples and Jews harbored resentment and animosity toward the Gentiles and Samaritans.[142]

We can translate these instructions into, "Go to those with whom we have a connection." Is this not what Jesus was saying to his disciples? The most important part of his instructions was that they would be empowered to deliver the good news.

We are all familiar with Acts 1:8: "But you will receive power when the Holy Spirit comes on you; and you will be my witnesses in Jerusalem, and in all Judea and Samaria, and to the ends of the earth." The Lord leaves no doubt. He defines the audience as everyone everywhere. But like Jesus in human form, he had both time and geographic limitations. He told his disciples they would do more than he could. They were to be his messengers to the world.

Where has God appointed you? To whom has God called you? As you pray for those who are unsaved, do you listen for the Lord's voice? Has he called you to connect with family and friends, acquaintances, or those with similar interests?

He Told Them What to Say

> "From that time Jesus began to preach, saying, "Repent, for the kingdom of heaven is at hand"..."And proclaim as you go, saying, 'The kingdom of heaven is at hand'" (Matt. 4:17; 10:7).

Essentially, their message was that salvation (access to the kingdom) was within their reach. He gave them words to say that would remind a Jewish audience of the message of the coming Messiah. Scripture is filled with examples of the Lord giving his servants the words to say: Moses, Joshua, and the prophets to mention a few. In these and other examples, these men did not have a clue of what to say. They needed divine knowledge and understanding. While we have a lot of tools at our fingertips, those tools need to be adapted to the situation where he places us.

Remember, we have within us the Holy Spirit who gives the words that resonate with the receiver. Therefore, we can share this timeless message with boldness and confidence. Our message by actions and words is that freedom from bondage and the penalty of sin is immediately available.

He Told Them What to Do

> "Heal the sick, raise the dead, cleanse lepers, cast out demons" (Matt. 10:1, 8a).

Just as the words needed for spiritual conversation are beyond our ability, so, too, are the actions Jesus expects us to do. He told his disciples to perform miracles, the same miracles that they had seen him do with ease. In essence, Jesus told his disciples to have compassion on the people, that is, meet their needs.

Mark tells us, "And they cast out many demons and anointed with oil many who were sick and healed them" (Mark 6:13).

Do we believe that we have the power within us to perform miracles? While some might deny that we can perform miracles today, God chose to demonstrate his power through us. We need to allow the Holy Spirit to work, and God will bring the result.

What is your grace gift? Where has God used you to meet needs in a given situation? Where is God using you to build up the body? Has the Lord given you a leadership gift?

He Told Them to Give Freely

> "You received without paying; give without pay"
> (Matt. 10:8b).

Jesus's miracles flowed freely, and he received nothing in return. Salvation is a gift. The transformed life is a gift. The abundant life is a gift. The indwelling Spirit is a gift. Since they are gifts, why would we expect compensation for exercising the power that he has given us.

He Told Them to Go Unencumbered

> "Do not get any gold or silver or copper to take with you in your belts—no bag for the journey or extra shirt or sandals or a staff, for the worker is worth his keep" (Matt. 10:9–10).

Jesus continued by giving instructions on what his disciples were to take with them on their travels. He told them to "go as you are."

First, he told them not to take (or acquire) money for their journey. Didn't they need money for food and lodging? Jesus commissioned them for his work; therefore, they were to trust that he would provide what was needed.

Second, they were not to be encumbered by taking extra belongings. But what if their sandals wore out or their staff broke? It would seem prudent to have spares. The idea here is that they should not worry about or be distracted by keeping up with extras.

Third, they were not to take the time to gather or acquire funds and extra supplies. They were to go with what they had. The command was "Go!"

Fourth, by traveling light, the people they encountered in the towns and villages might be more receptive to extending hospitality. The disciples were not to give the impression of self-sufficiency.

Fifth, by going with minimum provisions, they were less likely to draw the attention of thieves.

When Jesus sent out the seventy-two disciples, he instructed them to "greet no one." There is to be no delay, no stopping along the way, no idle conversation. Their focus was to be on advancing the gospel. It is difficult for us to take the gospel to those who are not like us.
In most cases, there needs to be some affinity, some common ground for the gospel to be planted effectively. To express this in an extreme: How can a homeless person hear what a man in a tuxedo or a woman in a ball gown is saying? Most of us do not have the gift of evangelism where the message is delivered without a second thought. Regardless, the command is to go!

He Told Them to Seek Receptive Ears

> Whatever town or village you enter, search there for some worthy person and stay at their house until you leave. As you enter the home, give it your greeting. If the home is deserving, let your peace rest on it; if it is not, let your peace return to you. If anyone will not welcome you or listen to your words, leave that home or town and shake the dust off your feet. Truly I tell you, it will be more bearable for Sodom and Gomorrah on the day of judgment than for that town (Matt. 10:11–15).

In the previous verses, Jesus told them they were to depend on the Lord. Here he explained that their needs would be met by those who welcomed the message they gave.

In essence, Jesus was giving his disciples instructions on how to find people who had "ears to hear." Hospitality would be an indication of acceptance.

When going into the home of a stranger, they were told to greet them. If the greeting was not received positively, they were to move on. Those rejecting their presence were responsible for their own spiritual well-being. When Jesus sent out the seventy-two (Luke 10:5), he gave them the customary greeting they were to use: "Peace be to this house!"

Ralph Neighbour, founder of TOUCH Outreach Ministries, states that there are two types of people: Type A are those who are receptive to the gospel, and Type B are those who either reject the message outright or show no interest.[143]

The Bible tells us that there are five types of fools: the simple, the silly, the sensual, the scorning, and the steadfast. The Word also tells us that we are to have nothing to do with the scorners—those who have embraced actions and thinking that are an abomination to God (Ps. 1:1) and avoid steadfast fools—those who are closed-minded and self-confident and are actively engaged in enlisting others to their thinking (Ps. 14:1).[144]

Throughout the history of Israel, there have been those who had the faith of Abraham and unfailingly anticipated the coming Messiah. On the other hand, many gave up. As Jesus sent the disciples to the Jews, we can assume that only those whose hearts were prepared and had "ears to hear."

To Review

Jesus told his disciples that they were to:

- Go with authority,
- Be empowered,
- Minister in pairs,
- Go to those who needed to hear the gospel,
- Use words given by the Lord,
- Show compassion (perform miracles) in the power of the Spirit,
- Be unencumbered,
- Seek receptive ears, and
- Leave when rejected.

Resources for Leading a Person to the Lord

- Four Spiritual Laws[145]
- Peace with God[146]
- The Master Plan of Evangelism[147]
- Turning Everyday Conversations into Gospel Conversations[148]
- Questioning Evangelism[149]

According to nineteenth-century English preacher, Charles Spurgeon, "Every Christian is either a missionary or an impostor."

Have you adopted Jesus's guidelines for reaching the lost and discipling believers?

Christ in Me: disciplined disciplemaking?

DISCIPLEMAKINC CHALLENGES

The Parable of the Soils[150]

> And he told them many things in parables, saying: "A sower went out to sow. And as he sowed, some seeds fell along the path, and the birds came and devoured them. Other seeds fell on rocky ground, where they did not have much soil, and immediately they sprang up, since they had no depth of soil, but when the sun rose they were scorched. And since they had no root, they withered away. Other seeds fell among thorns, and the thorns grew up and choked them. Other seeds fell on good soil and produced grain, some a hundredfold, some sixty, some thirty. He who has ears, let him hear" (Matt. 13:3–9).

In the parable of the Sower, Jesus presented a clear picture to people who were familiar with farming. While they grasped the images, they missed the spiritual application—even the disciples. When questioned about the meaning of the parable, Jesus quoted Isaiah indicating that there are various responses to truth.

> "And he said, "Go, and say to this people: Keep on hearing, but do not understand; keep on seeing, but do not perceive. Make the heart of this people dull, and their ears heavy, and blind their eyes; lest they see with their eyes, and hear with their ears, and understand with their hearts, and turn and be healed"' (Isa. 6:9–10).

He then goes on to reveal the meaning of the parable and the challenges of making disciples.

There are three elements to the parable:

The Seed

The seed is the gospel message, the Word, truth. Some believe that the custom of the time was to spread the seed and then return and plow it under. In spiritual terms, we are to share the gospel and then return and disciple the hearer. It is important to recognize that the one who spreads the seed may not be the one who tills, waters, or harvests the crop.

The Soil

The soil represents the heart of the person hearing the message. Jesus describes four types of soil or conditions of the heart: the path, stony ground, thorns, and good ground.

The Sower

The sower spreads the message across various soils. Jesus was talking about how his message would be received across the four responses or soils the sower could expect when sharing the gospel or discipling a believer. These include: the hardened heart (the path), shallow hearing (rocky places), the temptations of the world (thorns), and healthy growth (good soil).

The Path

> "And as he sowed, some seeds fell along the path, and the birds came and devoured them. When anyone hears the word of the kingdom and does not understand it, the evil one comes and snatches away what has been sown in his heart. This is what was sown along the path" (Matt. 13:4, 19).

The path was packed soil because it was heavily traveled, and nothing could grow. It went along or through an unfenced field. If the farmer plowed up the pathway, people made a new path, so the farmer would just leave it.

The seed could not grow because there was nothing to which the message could attach itself. The heart is hardened or unreceptive. This may be in the form of outright rejection, contrary thinking, or an unprepared heart. The message is blown away or quickly snatched by birds before it can take root. The hearer hurries on without reflecting on what was said. The soil (heart) does not receive the message, and therefore, the hearer gives no thought to it. Pastor-teacher John MacArthur calls this the unresponsive heart.

When discipling a hardened heart, we are commanded to spread the gospel without regard to where it lands. Because of that command, we send workers into creative access countries to minister to those with hardened hearts. These workers continue to sow the seed by building relationships, being Christ in an unbelieving community, and sharing and explaining the Word. Eventually, the seed falls on fertile soil and takes root.

On the other hand, What about us? The unresponsive heart we encounter may be a committed fool who is steadfast in their conviction that there is no God (Ps. 14:1) and whose intent is to turn us away from our own belief. Jesus stated that in these cases, we are to shake the dust from our feet and move on (Matt. 10:14). We are to avoid being influenced by another's faulty beliefs.

Then there are those who understand all too clearly what is required and are unwilling to pay the price. When we encounter hardened hearts, we are to build a relationship, move conversations toward spiritual matters, and share and explain the Word. We are to be Christ to these people. We need to cover our discipling relationships with prayer. We need to pray that the person's heart will soften, that the seed will take root, and that they will become receptive.

Rocky Places

Other seeds fell on rocky ground, where they did not
have much soil, and immediately they sprang up, since

they had no depth of soil, but when the sun rose they were scorched. And since they had no root, they withered away. ... When anyone hears the word of the kingdom and does not understand it, the evil one comes and snatches away what has been sown in his heart. This is what was sown along the path. As for what was sown on rocky ground, this is the one who hears the word and immediately receives it with joy, yet he has no root in himself, but endures for a while, and when tribulation or persecution arises on account of the word, immediately he falls away (Matt. 13:5, 19–21).

It is likely that the farmer had cultivated the field over several years and plowed up and removed most of the rocks in the field. However, in Palestine, there is often limestone below the surface of the soil.

Jesus said that under this condition, the message was received and immediately took root. However, because of the rocky places or rock under the soil, the root system was inadequate to sustain growth in response to the message. The person may appear to be spiritually healthy, but when trials and tribulation come, the message fades and does not sustain the person through difficulties. MacArthur calls this the preoccupied heart. The concept is a shallow hearing of the Word, an inability to give serious thought to the message, and a failure to begin the journey of faith. There is no transforming work.

When discipling a stony heart, the disciple's responsibility is to come alongside the believer and help them shore up their faith to help them navigate the difficulties of life. The disciplemaking process is one of living life alongside this person and exemplify a life of faith in times of difficulty. That is, living out and giving testimony to the power of the gospel.

Thorns

"Other seeds fell among thorns, and the thorns grew up and choked them. As for what was sown among thorns, this is the one who hears the word, but the cares of the world and the deceitfulness of riches choke the word, and it proves unfruitful" (Matt. 13:7, 22).

It is very likely that the farmer was diligent in removing the weeds from his field but may have left roots. Moreover, the wind carried seeds in from nearby weeds. Weeding is a never-ending process. Kristi, my daughter-in-law, defines a weed as anything that grows where it is not wanted. Jesus stated that the weeds were already in the field and grew, keeping the good seed from growing. He described weeds as the temptations of the world. He said that believers will fall to temptation and be prevented from being productive members of the kingdom. From the initial hearing of the gospel, the believer loses focus and is blown about by the winds of the world. MacArthur calls this the impulsive heart. Again, there is no transforming work taking place.

When discipling a thorny heart, as with the stony heart, the disciplemaker must live a life that is free from the distractions of the world. Again, he or she must be Christ to one who is sidetracked. That means establishing a relationship, sharing testimonies about victory over challenges and the freedom that comes from a life of faith. The disciple should consider connecting the thorny-hearted person with someone who has overcome related worldly distractions.

Like the farmer who plants annually or biannually, the disciple maker must be persistent in sowing seed by his or her presence or by bringing the Word into a relevant situation. Above all, in these difficult situations, we need to be patient, gently persistent, proceed with prayer, and operate under the power of the Holy Spirit. Finally, there may come a time when the disciple needs to move on. This decision should not be based on the difficulty in discipling but on the leading of the Holy Spirit.

Good Ground

> "Other seeds fell on good soil and produced grain, some a hundredfold, some sixty, some thirty As for what was sown on good soil, this is the one who hears the word and understands it. He indeed bears fruit and yields, in one case a hundredfold, in another sixty, and in another thirty" (Matt. 13:9, 23).

When the message falls on fertile soil, there is a threefold response: First, the person eagerly seeks the truth and, and as a result, becomes a productive member of the family of God. This is the believer who actively seeks more. They are enthusiastic about being discipled and growing in the Lord. They are open, focused, willing to learn, and energized by the Word. Second, the person begins to demonstrate the fruit of the Spirit. Third, the person is willing to engage in sharing the gospel and leading others to a deeper life. Ultimately, they bear fruit.

Jesus indicated differences in fruitfulness. The quantity of the fruit depends on how much the hearer surrenders to the power of the Spirit, responds to God's call, and willingness to take faithful risks. Nonetheless, all bear fruit. Pastor John MacArthur calls this the well-prepared heart.

In discipling an open heart there is no better place to begin than with the Word. A pastor friend has compiled ten to twelve Scripture verses dealing with each of six basics of the faith:

1. The Bible
2. God
3. People
4. Jesus
5. Salvation
6. Discipleship

Discipling Resources

Disciple makers often use materials with which they were discipled. A friend of mine was discipled using the Ten Transferable Concepts from Cru (Campus Crusade for Christ).[151] I prefer to use materials by the Christian Mentors Network. This material covers thirty-six topics ranging from spiritual, personal, and lifestyle characteristics of a godly life.[152] Other excellent resources are available through Intervarsity Christian Fellowship and the Navigators.[153]

Discipling requires being observant, available, intentional, and prepared. The real work of discipling is done by the Holy Spirit by preparing the heart of the disciple and the heart of the person being discipled by the Word and conversation. The Lord will advance his kingdom, but he wants to do so through you and me. It is important to remember that when the Lord wants you to do something, he will do it. One of the best ways to learn to disciple is to be discipled, that is, through learning by example, observing the Holy Spirit working through the one discipling you, and experiencing the Holy Spirit at work in you.

"Not by might, nor by power, but by my Spirit, says the Lord of hosts" (Zech. 4:6).

Do you test the soil before attempting to disciple others?

Christ in me: knowing who is ready.

MENTORING

"You then, my child, be strengthened by the grace that is in Christ Jesus, and what you have heard from me in the presence of many witnesses entrust to faithful men, who will be able to teach others also. Share in suffering as a good soldier of Christ Jesus" (2 Tim. 2:1–2).

Pulpit ministry, Sunday school, and small groups are standard ways for providing instruction in the faith. The teaching imparts one message to many. The smaller the group, the more tailored the message can be and the more opportunity for personalizing. On the other hand, mentoring, or one-to-one discipling, is the most effective method. This is teaching that is tailored to the individual being discipled. It is one believer pouring his or her life into another believer.

Mentoring in the Bible

While mentoring is not a biblical word, we see many examples in Scripture. Joseph got to be the faithful, obedient servant of the Lord under his father. Remember, he left home as a teenager. We see Joshua taking the reins of leadership after forty years under Moses's leadership. Normally we do not think about Paul needing mentoring, yet it was Barnabas who brought Paul to Antioch in

Mentoring in the Bible
• Jacob and Joseph
• Moses and Joshua
• Eli and Samuel
• Elijah and Elisha
• Bamabas and Paul
• Paul and Timothy
• Paul and Titus

Acts chapter eleven. For the next two chapters, it is Barnabas and Paul, and then in chapter thirteen, the team became Paul and Barnabas. You can probably add your own examples to this list.

The Purpose of Mentoring

The purpose of mentoring is to develop disciplemakers. Mentoring is advancing the kingdom one person at a time.

The Mentoring Process

Mentoring begins with Spirit-direction and a relationship. A man mentioned something he was struggling with in our small group. It was something I had dealt with. I was motivated to build a relationship and pour my life into his. It was a call. Mentoring can be an iron sharpens iron relationship or sharing life experiences with a less mature believer or a non-believer. Mentoring can be for spiritual growth or the development of ministry skills. As mentoring is one life being poured into another life, it is the Spirit who leads, guides, and directs. Mentoring is most effective when there is openness and honesty in the conversation. This honesty opens the door to personal transformation, which leads to transformed marriages, families, relationships, churches, and so on. Mentoring is only effective when the Spirit leads. That means the mentor must bathe the relationship in prayer and allow the Spirit to speak through him or her. This takes patience. For some, it is a slow process. I built a relationship with a man for seven years before he prayed for salvation. The Lord said, "Keep on."

Then there are times when there is no growth. Things to watch for are:

- Not being prepared
- Misplacing the study book
- Eyes glazing over
- Failure to keep appointments

In such cases, "shake the dust from your sandals."

Mentoring Resource

See the resources mentioned above in the parable of the Soils, page 151

MY JOURNEY TO DISCIPLEMAKING

Before describing my journey to disciple-making, I need to make two important points.

The first is a question: Where is the line between my role in my salvation and the work of the Spirit? Of course, I know I made the decision to accept Christ as my Savior. But is that true? As discussed in the first chapter, it is the work of the Holy Spirit to convict us of sin, judgment, and righteousness. I remember that week at summer camp, seeing leaders ministering and listening to lessons. Then on the last evening, there must have been Spirit-inspired words at the campfire. The more I think about my role, the less credit I can take for that decision. It was the work of the Spirit.

Second, I was wandering through life looking for something to satisfy the emptiness in me. On that Lay Witness weekend, there were the Spirit-filled testimonies of people, the words they used, and thoughts that apparently resonated with me and prepared me for the question: "Have you given Jesus control of your life?" I did not stop to think. My response was an automatic "no" followed by a willingness to surrender to the Lord. Again, where was the line between the prompting of the Spirit and my decision? It is in our DNA to be in control of our lives. Therefore, I cannot take credit for that decision. It was the work of the Spirit.

Following that line of thinking, I cannot take credit for my disciple-making journey and the lives that have been changed because of my words, presence, or actions. What follows is a description of how the Spirit led and equipped me for teaching and mentoring and motivated me to make a difference in the lives of others.

Teaching: At some point, the Spirit led someone to ask me to teach a Sunday school class. Since that time, I have been teaching classes and leading small groups. I have a passion for getting into the Word, researching the context, and doing word studies. Moreover, I am amazed when the Lord inserts himself into the lesson beyond my preparation. This is the work of the Spirit.

Evangelizing: The thought of sharing the gospel terrified me. To make it worse, I knew it was something I was supposed to do. A friend encouraged me to go through Evangelism Explosion (EE). During the course, I saw two people come to the Lord. Then I saw my father come to the Lord. Then a friend came to the Lord. I am not an evangelist. I have forgotten most of what I learned in EE, but the concepts and Scriptures come to mind when needed. I am confident that the Spirit will continue to use me to lead others into his kingdom. This is the work of the Spirit.

Counseling: At one point I believed that the Lord was leading me to be a pastor, and I took a course in biblical counseling from Dr. Larry Crabb. But being a pastor was not a part of the Lord's plan for me. However, I find places to use Crabb's concepts in teaching and mentoring.

Mentoring: Several years ago, the Lord led me to mentor two men. Since that time, I try to mentor at least two or three men. I draw from my own life experiences the Word, a book, or topical study relating to the needs of the man, his spiritual maturity, and the issues with which he is dealing. However, it is the Holy Spirit who puts it all together. Mentoring is action directed by the Spirit.

I am a planner. That is how the Lord wired me. I like things laid out logically and clearly. It is the way I think. But what I have described above was never in my plan. It has evolved over time. The common thread in all of this is the direction of the Holy Spirit. He gives me eyes to see and ears to hear. He gives me words to say. He gives me Scriptures or biblical concepts to use. Then there are times when nothing comes to mind in preparing for a meeting but the right words and ideas flow in conversations, nonetheless. Amazing! The Spirit is the one who does the work. He does the heavy lifting. He is *"the wind beneath my wings."*[154]

Look, I tell you, lift up your eyes, and see that the fields are white for harvest. Already the one who reaps is receiving wages and gathering fruit for eternal life, so that sower and reaper may rejoice together. For here the saying holds true, "One sows and another reaps." I sent you to reap that for which you did not labor. Others have labored, and you have entered into their labor (John 4:35–38).

Where have you seen the Spirit working through you? Has the Lord used you to make a difference in the lives of others?

Disciplemaking: Not I but Christ in me.

LIVING OUT OUR CALLING

> As each has received a gift, use it to serve one another, as good stewards of God's varied grace: whoever speaks, as one who speaks oracles of God; whoever serves, as one who serves by the strength that God supplies—in order that in everything God may be glorified through Jesus Christ. To him belong glory and dominion forever and ever. Amen (1 Pet. 4:10–11).

We Are Called to Salvation

"*J*esus replied, 'I tell you the truth, unless you are born again, you cannot see the Kingdom of God'" (John 3:3).

The Problem: At birth, we were wired to follow our own path, pursue our own goals, and do what is right in our own eyes. That inevitably leads to conflicts with others who are wired the same way. We focus on whatever attracts us at the moment in an attempt to fill the emptiness in our lives. When we live for ourselves, we fail, often with disastrous results in relationships, health, and productivity. English writer, philosopher, and lay theologian G. K. Chesterton, in response to the question, "What is wrong with the world?" said, "I am." The bottom line: We are lost.

The Solution: God has a plan for me, "not for evil [but] to give you a future and a hope" (Jer. 29:11). God's plan is for us to follow his path, not our own. The problem is that we do not have within us the ability to follow God's individually designed path for us. We cannot save ourselves. Recall that it is the Holy Spirit who convicts us of sin, righteousness, and judgment. It is his Spirit who prompts us to accept God's offer of salvation. It is a choice: God's path to eternal life or the path to eternal death. It is the Spirit of God that leads us to the throne of grace and salvation. A pastor friend said that we have absolutely nothing to do with our salvation; we have everything to do with our damnation.

We Are Called to Commitment

> "Therefore, if anyone is in Christ, he is a new creation. The old has passed away; behold, the new has come" (2 Cor. 5:17).

The Problem: The pre-salvation way of thinking and behaving continues after salvation. While we may have the assurance of salvation, we find it impossible to break away from the old life. The old patterns of thinking and behavior persist.

The Solution: God corrected this problem by placing his Holy Spirit in us. He began the process of making us new. While he places his Spirit in us at salvation, it is not until we agree to allow that Spirit to live out new patterns of thinking and behavior that we experience real change. It is a matter of commitment, submission, and surrender. While we may remember the moment we gave the Lord control of our lives, it was the Spirit who inspired us to make that decision. It is the Spirit of God within us that brings spiritual transformation.

We are Called to a Deeper Life.

> "We know that our old self was crucified with him [Jesus] in order that the body of sin might be brought to nothing, so that we would no longer be enslaved to sin" (Rom. 6:6).

The Problem: The Spirit leads us to sense that there is more to the Christian life than what we gain through a "normal" relationship with the Lord. Perhaps we encounter a barrier that is insurmountable.

Perhaps we feel a gnawing desire for a closer walk with the Lord, or there may be a challenge that we cannot overcome.

The Solution: Having experienced spiritual transformation, we recognize that there is a power that can take us deeper in our relationship with the Lord. We realize at the Spirit level that there is much more to "Christ in me" than we are experiencing. Therefore, it is a matter of making a deeper commitment. It is the Spirit of God who elevates our faith to new levels.

We Are Uniquely Equipped to Serve the Lord

> "To each is given the manifestation of the Spirit for the common good" (1 Cor. 12:7).

The Problem: God calls us to do things beyond our training, wisdom, and skills. We cannot achieve eternal life on our own. Nor can we commit to a power greater than ourselves on our own. Therefore, it follows that we cannot advance his kingdom on our own. We understand and engage in our calling without results or real productivity.

The Solution: "Christ in me," the Holy Spirit, equips us to make a difference in the world. He gives us grace gifts, gifts tailored to the situations before us, gifts to build the body, and gifts to lead the body. By being available and equipped, we see God at work bringing people to the throne of grace, spiritual transformation to others, building his church, and advancing his kingdom. He wants to work through us. It is critical to understand that God's call and equipping is unique to each of us. Because of "Christ in me," we cannot claim success in transformation or making a difference in the lives of others. It is God who does it; therefore, he gets the credit. It is the Spirit of God that equips us supernaturally to do the impossible for God.

We Are Uniquely Called to Make Disciples

> And Jesus came and said to them, "All authority in heaven and on earth has been given to me. Go

therefore and make disciples of all nations, baptizing them in the name of the Father and of the Son and of the Holy Spirit, teaching them to observe all that I have commanded you. And behold, I am with you always, to the end of the age" (Matt. 28:18–20).

The Problem: We experience an inner nagging of the Spirit to lead others to Christ, to make disciples, and to build his church. We see needs but do not feel capable of meeting those needs. We fear how people will respond to us. Therefore, we do not attempt to engage in our God-given calling.

The Solution: We are correct in our belief that we cannot do what God is asking us to do. The Lord wants us to step aside and get out of his way. He is the one who does the work. He wants to work through us using the spiritual gifts he has given us. It is critical to understand that our calling to make disciples where he has planted us and for those he brings across our path. It is the Spirit who does the work of transforming lives.

We Are Called and Equipped to Make a Difference in the Lives of Others

"For we are his workmanship, created in Christ Jesus for good works, which God prepared beforehand, that we should walk in them" (Eph. 2:10).

The Problem: People are hurting. They need salvation. Believers need spiritual transformation, encouragement, physical and spiritual healing, and be set free from their objections and excuses. The world is a mess. Our churches are a mess.

The Solution: God has uniquely called, equipped, and empowered each of us to advance his kingdom. He has transformed us, and therefore, we are different from our culture. He will make a difference in the lives of others through us. He has empowered us to change the world he has laid out for us. God is the solution to the problems of the world. His plan is to work through me and you to do that. The solution lies in our availability. It is the Spirit who makes a difference in the lives of others.

Christ in Me: the power to make a difference.

"Then he said to me, 'Not by might, nor by power, but by my Spirit, says the Lord of hosts'" (Zech. 4:6).

"I can do all things through him who strengthens me" (Phil. 4:13).

ACKNOWLEDGMENTS

I appreciate the time and attention that Rev. Robert Young and Rev. Fred King have given in reviewing this work. Additionally, their input into my life has found its way into many of these pages. I also deeply appreciate the time and attention of my wife, Linda, my daughter, Diane, and friend, Trish Rollins, whose careful reading, editing, and content suggestions have contributed significantly to this volume. I am indebted to Steve Bracken for suggesting changes and refinements to clarify the message of this work. Finally, I owe a great deal of gratitude to the team at Xulon Press for their editing, suggestions, design, and encouragement. They have made my efforts presentable.

ABOUT THE AUTHOR

*L*es Tripp is a ministry leader in his church and a certified men's ministry coach. He has led ministry to men in three churches and served for ten years on the men's ministry leadership team of the Christian and Missionary Alliance. He has also served as a regional men's ministry coordinator. His passion is for discipling men. He provides men's disciplemaking resources on www.mensdisciplemaking.org and is the author of *Strong and Courageous: A devotional for Men in the Battle,* as well as the book *Walls and Gates: A devotional Study of the Book of Nehemiah.*

Les spent twenty-three years in the US Air Force in the field of information technology. He served in various command and staff positions. He spent another seventeen years working for a defense contractor.

Les and his wife, Linda, live in Cantonment, Florida, and have three children and nine grandchildren.

NOTES

ENDNOTES

1   Elmer Towns, *Understanding the Deeper Life: A Guide to Christian Experience*, (Old Tappan, New Jersey: Fleming H. Revell, 1988), 18–19.

2   Eugene Peterson, A Long Obedience in the Same Direction: Discipleship in an Instant Society, (Downers Grove: InterVarsity Press, 2000).

3   R. Laird Harris, Gleason L Archer, Jr., and Bruce K. Waltke, *Theological Wordbook of the Old Testament*, (Chicago: Moody Press, 1980), Vol. 1, 497.

4   *The New Brown, Driver and Briggs (BDB) Hebrew and English Lexicon of the Old Testament*, (Lafayette, IN: Associated Publishers and Authors, 1981), 559–60 (2b); Lawrence O. Richards, *Expository Dictionary of Bible Words*, (Grand Rapids: Zondervan: 1985), 406–7; Harris, et al, Vol. 1, 496–497.

5   Frank E. Gaebelein, ed., *Expositor's Bible Commentary*, (Zondervan\Pradis\Pradis.exe, version 9.1. Genesis 3:22

6   Harris, et.al., Vol. 1, 497.

7   Gaebelein, Genesis 3:16.

8   Gaeblein, Job 19:25; Richards, 526–7.

9   American Heritage Dictionary, https://ahdictionary.com/, 10/26/2015.

10   Walter A. Ewell, ed., *Evangelical Dictionary of Theology*, (Grand Rapids: Baker, 1984), 262; W. E. Vine, *Expository Dictionary of New Testament* Word, (McLean, VA: McDonald Publishing, 1966), 226–227; Colin Brown, ed., *The New International Dictionary of New Testament Theology (DNTT)*, Vol 1, (Grand Rapids: Zondervan, 1971), 344–348; http://www.biblestudytools.com/dictionary/confession/, *Eaton's Bible Dictionary (10/2016)*; Richards, 183.

11   Vine, 961-3; Moody Theological Seminary, *New Testament Greek Lexicon – King James Version,* http://www.biblestudytools. com/ lexicons/greek/kjv/, (4/2012); Brown, *DNTT,* Vol. 1, 357–9; Millard

J. Erickson, Christian Theology, (Grand Rapids: Baker, 1985), 932– 40; Richards, 522; Ewell, 272–273; Gaebelein, John 3:5.

12   Joseph Thayer, QuickVerse 3.0, (FindEX.com, 2005-2009, *gennao*

and *anothen*).

13   Gaebelein, John 3:4.

14   Gaebalein, John 3:5.

15   Gaebelein, John 3:9.

16   Thayer, *pneuma.*

17   Thayer, *apollumi.*

18   Thayer, *aionios* and *zoe.*

19   Holman, Notes on John 3:16-18, 1782.

20   Wikopedia, http://en.wikipedia.org/wiki/RMS_Titanic, 5/8/2012.

21   Joel R. Green, Scot McKnight, and I. Howard Marshall, *Dictionary of Jesus and the Gospels,* (Downers Grove: Intervarsity, 1992),

604-5; Brown, *DNTT,* Vol. 2, 776–783; Richards, 479–481; Efriam Goldstein, *A Study on Biblical Concepts of Peace in the Old and New Testaments,* http://www.jewsforjesus.org/publications/ newsletter/1997_12/studyonbiblical, 11/30/1997; Elwell, 833.

22   Thayer, *eirena.*

23   Towns, 130.

24   Chris Lukes, "The Secret That Will Change Your Life," https:// www.christianitytoday.com/iyf/hottopics/faithvalues/8c6030.ht ml.

25   C. S. Lewis, *Mere Christianity,* (New York: HarperCollins, 2001), 50.

26   The NKJV translates the Greek word *meno* as "abide" in verses 3 and 4 and as "remain" in verses 5–8. The ESV uses "abide"

throughout.

27   George P. Pardington, *The Crisis of the Deeper Life*, (New York: Christian Alliance Publishing, 1925), 66–67.

28   Summarized from: Larry Crabb, *Basic Principles of Biblical Counseling*, (Grand Rapids: Zondervan, 1975).

29   https://billygraham.org/story/surviving-in-the-furnace-of-adversity/, 1/19/2021.

30   Thoughts on biblical peace based on the following resources: Elwell, 833; Green, et al., 604-5; Richards, 479-481; Goldstein, https://jewsforjesus.org/publications/newsletter/newsletter-dec- 1997/a-study-on-biblical-concepts-of-peace-in-the-old-and-new- testaments/, 11/30/1997.

31   Thayer, *eirena*.

32   Charles H. Spurgeon, "The Valley of the Shadow of Death," *THE JOURNAL OF BIBLICAL COUNSELING*, Vol. 18, No. 3, 2000, 34.

33   Rest is a common theme in the Bible. It is defined as a state of inner peace or security. The Hebrew word for rest is *noah*. It means the guaranteed continuance of hope and the assurance of being with the Lord in eternity. *Noah* is an instrument of deliverance; a place or position in which to settle down, a home. It means rest and salvation. Rest is knowing the presence of the Lord. It is, however, the Lord who gives rest. It is not something we achieve on our own (Joshua 1:15). Note that the giving of rest is a continuing process, not a one-time event. Richards, 524-5; BDB, 628c; Harris, et. al., Vol. 2, 562.

34   Crosswalk.com, https://www.crosswalk.com/faith/spiritual-life/ what-you-need-to-know-about-the-meaning-of-submission-in- the-bible.html, 11/1/2019.

35   Adapted from Bill Bright, *Have You Made the Wonderful Discovery of the Spirit-filled Life?* Campus Crusade for Christ, 1966, 12.

36   Towns, 20.

37   A. W. Tozer, *What is the Deeper Life*, https://www.cmalliance.org/alife/what-is-the-deeper-life, 9/28/2019.

38   *Ibid.*

39   Summarized from: Tozer, *The Deeper Life: Sustaining our relationship with God through Christ*, (Camp Hill: Christian Publications, 1997).

40   Pardington, 23.

41   Henry and Richard Blackaby, *Fresh Encounter: Experiencing God's Power for Spiritual Awakening*, (Nashville: Lifeway, 2019), 98.

42   Towns, 7-8.

43   https://visionchristianfamily.org/devotions/dev-year1/dev-year1- may/day-26-a-heart-strangely-warmed/, 10/24/2020.

44   Dietrich Bonhoeffer, *The Cost of Discipleship* (London: SCM Press, 1948/2001), 44.

45   Michael Cromate, "No Calling without a Caller," *Books and Culture*, July/August 1998, 16.

46   *Ibid*.

47   Oz Guinness, *The Call: Finding and Fulfilling the Central Purpose of your Life*, (Word Publishing: Nashville, 1998), 46.

48   https://www.merriam-webster.com/dictionary/success, 2/24/2020.

49   https://www.biblestudytools.com/dictionary/content-contentment/, 10/19/2019.

50   Towns, 176.

51   Towns, 178.

52   Oswald Chambers, *My Utmost for His Highest*, (New York: Dodd, Mead, & Co., 1935), 297.

53   Pardington, 99.

54   *John Piper Says He Longs for John Stott's Ambition, Discernment*, Christian Post, April 29, 2012, https://www.christianpost.com/ news/john-piper-says-he-longs-for-john-stotts-ambition- discernment.html, 11/4/2019.

55   This chapter on spiritual gifts was developed and expanded from a Bible study given by Rev. Robert Young, Ensley Alliance Church, Pensacola, Florida, Summer 2008.

56   R. E. Ciampa, and B. S. Rosner, *The First Letter to the*

Corinthians, (Grand Rapids: Erdmans, 2010), 573.

57 M. R. Vincent, *Word studies in the New Testament,* (New York: Charles Scribner's Sons, 1887), Vol. 3, 255.

58 Leon Morris, *1 Corinthians: An Introduction and Commentary,* (Downers Grove: InterVarsity Press, 1985), 164; R. L. Pratt,. Jr., *I & II Corinthians,* (Nashville: B&H Publishers, 2000), 214; David. Prior, *The Message of 1 Corinthians: Life in the Local Church,* (Downers Grove: InterVarsity Press, 1985), 196; A. F. Johnson, *1 Corinthians,* (Westmont, IL: IVP Academic, 2004), 219-20; Mark Taylor, *1 Corinthians,* (Nashville: B&H Publishers, 2014), 287; Ciampa and Rosner, 567–8.

59 Morris, *1 Corinthians,* 164; Pratt, 214; Prior, 196–7; Ciampa and Rosner, 570.

60 Morris, *1 Corinthians,* 164–5; Pratt, 214; Prior, 197; Ciampa and Rosner, 570–1.

61 Morris, *1 Corinthians,* 165; Pratt, 215; Prior, 197–8; Johnson, 220; Ciampa and Rosner, 571–2.

62 Leon Morris, *The Epistle to the Romans,* (Grand Rapids: Eerdmans; Inter-Varsity Press, 1988), 440; R. H. Mounce, *Romans,* (Nashville: Broadman & Holman Publishers, 1995), 234; J. R. W. Stott, *The Message of Romans: God's Good News for the World,* (Downers Grove: InterVarsity Press, 2001), 326; R. Mohrlang, Gerald L. Borchert, *Cornerstone Biblical Commentary, Vol. 14: Romans and Galatians,* (Carol Stream, IL: Tyndale House Publishers, 2007), 186; R. G. Gruenler, "Romans" in *Evangelical Commentary on the Bible,* (Grand Rapids: Baker Book House, 1995), Vol. 3, 950; Brown, D., A. R. Fausset and R. Jamieson, *A Commentary, Critical, Experimental, and Practical, on the Old and New Testaments: Acts–Revelation,* (London: William Collins, Sons, & Company, Limited, n.d.), Vol. 6, 264–5.

63 G. R. Osborne, *Romans,* (Downers Grove: InterVarsity Press, 2004), 326; Ken Boa and W. Kruidenier, *Romans,* (Nashville, TN: Broadman & Holman Publishers, 2000), 370.

64 Vincent, 154–155.

65   Transliteration of the Greek is provided to make a distinction between similar but different gifts. The transliteration is based on the Bible Hub interlinear New Testament, (https://biblehub.com/ interlinear/genesis/1-1.htm). Analysis of Greek words is based on A. L. Lukaszewski, M. Dubis, and J. T. Blakley, *The Lexham Syntactic Greek New Testament, SBL Edition: Exp ansions and Annotations*, (Bellingham, WA: Lexham Press, 2011).

66   Stott, *Romans*, 327; Ewell, 1044.

67   Vine, 903; Vincent, Vol. 3, 256; Elwell, 887, 1044; Johnson, 224–225; Brown, *DNTT*, Vol. 3, 74–76, 84; Ciampa and Rosner, 580–581, 610–11.

68   Stott, *Romans*, 327.

69   1 Corinthians 12:28; 14:40.

70   Vine, 903; John Phillips, *Exploring Romans*, (Moody, Chicago: 1969), 194; Richards, 507.

71   Elwell, 1045; Vincent, Vol. 3, 156; J. A. Witmer, *Romans*, (Vol. 2 of *The Bible Knowledge Commentary: An Exposition of the Scriptures*), (Wheaton: Victor Books, 1985), 488.

72   Vine, 1031; Phillips, 194; Vincent, Vol. 3, 157; Morris, *Romans*, 439-40; Osborne, https://ref.ly/logosres/ivntrm?ref=Bible.Ro12.3-8&off=8134&ctx=o+serve+themselves.%0a~2.+Serving.+This+cou326–7.

73   Osborne, 326-327; Vine, 1131; H. C. G. Moule, *Studies in Romans*, (Grand Rapids: Kregel Publications, 1977), 209; Phillips 194.

74   Vine, 1134; Moule, 209; Phillips, 194; Osborne, 327.

75   *Ibid*.

76   Vine, 1134; Phillips, 195; Osborne, 327-328; Elwell, 1044; Vincent, Vol. 3, 157; Millard J. Erickson, *Concise Dictionary of Christian Theology*, (Grand Rapids: Baker,1986), 53.

77   *Ibid*.

78   Erickson, *Dictionary*, 64; Richards, 309; Moule, 209; Phillips, 195.

79   *Ibid.*

80   Vincent, 158; Henry, Matthew, *Commentary on the Whole Bible* (One Volume), (Grand Rapids: Zondervan,1961), 1786; Phillips, 195; Richards, 403, 538; Elwell, 810–811; Osborne, 328; Brown, *DNTT*, Vol. 1, 164; Mounce, 235.

81   *Ibid.*

82   Phillips, 196; Moule,196; Richards, 440; Morris, *Romans*, 442; Osborne, 328–9.

83   *Ibid.*

84   Johnson, 215–216.

85   Prior, 199.

86   Ciampa and Rosner, 576–581; Pratt, 214; Prior, 195–197; Johnson, 219–220; Morris, *1 Corinthians*, 167-8.

87   Erickson, *Theology*, 881.

88   Walter Bauer, Fredrick W. Danker, William F. Arndt, and F. Wilber Gingrich, *A Greek-English Lexicon of the New Testament and Other Early Christian Literature*, (Chicago: University of Chicago Press, 1979), 759d; Pratt, 215; Ciampa, 574; Johnson, 221.

89   Eugene G. Givens, *The Holy Spirit: His Gifts and Power are for You*, (Woodbridge, VA: Dr. Eugene G. Givens, 2011), 60-61. In writing about spiritual gifts, Givens focuses on the nine situation gifts. He provides examples of how the Spirit worked through him in a number of situations. He does not give examples of the gifts of prophesy, tongues or interpretation of tongues, however.

90   Bauer, et al., 164a; Morris, *1 Corinthians*, 165; Pratt, 215; Henry, 1819; Ciampa, 574–577.

91   Words of Knowledge: https://www.blueletterbible.org/Comm/ smith_chuck/HolySpirit/hs_15.cfm, 6/1/2020.

92   Givens, 69.

93   Bauer, et al., 664; Gaebelein, 1 Corinthians 12:9; Pratt, 215; Ciampa, 577–578.

94   Givens, 104-5.

95   Morris, 166; Ciampa, 578; Johnson, 222–224.

96   Givens, 114-5.

97   Vine, 757; Ewell, 723–4; Bauer, et al, 208a; Richards, 444–445; Prior, 206-7; Brown, *DNTT*, Vol. 2, 605; Pratt, 221; Erickson, *Theology*, 409.

98   Young study notes.

99   Source: International worker in a creative access country.

100   Givens, 131-2.

101   Prophesy in the church today: https://churchleaders.com/ outreach-missions/outreach-missions-articles/338040-what-does-prophecy-look-like-today.html, 6/1/2020.

102   Vincent, Vol. 3, 256; Henry, 1819; Ciampa, 574; Morris, *1 Corinthians*, 167.

103   Prior, 208-209; Johnson, 225–226; Ciampa, 582.

104   Givens, 82-83.

105   Gaebelein, 1 Cor 12:10; D. K. Lowery, "1 Corinthians" in J. F. Walvoord and R. B. Zuck (eds.), *The Bible Knowledge Commentary: An Exposition of the Scriptures*, (Wheaton: Victor Books, 1985), Vol. 2, 533; Pratt, 216–217; Brown, *DNTT*, Vol. 3, 1078–1081; Morris, *1 Corinthians*, 167–168; Prior, 200.

106   As a foreign language or dialect: Gaebelein, 1 Cor 12:10; Lowery, 533; Pratt, 216–217; Brown, *DNTT*, Vol. 3, 1078-1081; Morris, *1 Corinthians*, 167-168; Prior, 200; as an ecstatic utterance: Elwell, 1045; Ciampa, 585; Erickson, *Theology*, 855-856, 877-882.

107   Johnson, 227.

108   Lowery, 533; Pratt, 217; Morris, *1 Corinthians*, 167–168; Brown, *DNTT*, Vol. 3,1080.

109   Morris, *1 Corinthians*, 172; D. L. Adkins in E. A. Blum, and T. Wax, (eds.), *CSB Study Bible: Notes*, (Nashville: Holman Bible Publishers, 2017), 1829–30.

110   Pratt, 220–224.

111   Ciampa, 609; Gaebelein, 1 Corinthians 12:28; W. Baker, *1 Corinthians*, (Carol Stream: Tyndale House Publishers, 2009), 185.

112 Young study notes.

113 Richards, 59–60; Elwell, 70-72; Prior, 217–219; Ciampa, 610;
     H. W. Hoehner, *Ephesians*, Vol. 2 in Walvoord and Zuck,
     eds., *The Bible Knowledge Commentary: An Exposition of
     the Scriptures*, (Wheaton: Victor Books, 1985), 635.

114 Pratt, 220; Prior, 217–9; Johnson, 236–7.

115 Barnabas: (Acts 14:14); James: (Galatians 1:19); Silas and
     Timothy: (1 Thessalonians 2:6); Andronicus and Junias:
     (Romans 16:7); Johnson 236–237; Taylor, 301–302; Pratt,
     220.

116 Richards, 507; Elwell, 887; Brown, *DNTT*, Vol. 3, 74–76, 84;
     Ciampa, 610–611.

117 Richards, 507.

118 Brown, *DNTT*, Vol. 3, 89, Taylor, 302.

119 Elwell, 1045; Ciampa, 585; Erickson, *Theology*, 855–856,
     877-882.

120 Morris, *1 Corinthians*, 172-3; Pratt, 220; Prior, 219; Johnson,
     238; Taylor, 302; Ciampa, 611–12.

121 Vincent, 260; Lowery, 534; E. W. Bullinger, *The
     Companion Bible: Being the Authorized Version of 1611
     with the Structures and Notes, Critical, Explanatory and
     Suggestive and with 198 Appendixes*. (Bellingham, WA:
     Faithlife 2018), Vol. 1, 1717.

122 Vine, 544; Pratt, 221; Elwell, 1043; Erickson, *Dictionary*, 72.

123 Vine, 553; Vincent, 260; Elwell, 1040; Pratt, 221; Prior, 220–
     1; Johnson, 238; Ciampa, 613; Taylor, 300–301; Morris, *1
     Corinthians*, 173.

124 Vincent, 260; Richards, 19-20; Elwell, 1043; Brown, *DNTT*,
     Vol. 1, 198; Prior, 223–4; Johnson, 238; Ciampa, 613–4.

125 Ciampa, 614.

126 Vine, 608; Brown, *DNTT*, Vol. 1, 581–2.

127 Pratt, 221; Johnson, 238–9.

128 Johnson, 238-9; Prior, 223–4; Ciampa, 614-618; Taylor, 320.

129 Lowery, 534-5; Johnson, 238-9; Ciampa, 614-618; Prior,

223–4.

130 Vine, 384; Elwell, 1045; F. Foulkes, *Ephesians: An Introduction and Commentary*, (Downers Grove: InterVarsity, 1989), 125; Vincent, 382; M. Anders, *Galatians-Colossians*, (Nashville: Boardman and Holman, 1999), 162.

131 Foulkses, 123-6; Anders, 161-2; W. L. Liefeld, *Ephesians*, (Downers Grove: InterVarsity, 1997), Ephesians 4:11; Hoehner, 634-5.

132 Vine, 1042; Brown, *DNTT*, Vol. 3, 564-8; Stott, 164–6; Liefeld, Eph. 4:11.

133 Hoehner, 635; Foulkes, 126; Anders, 151-3, 161–2; Liefeld, Eph. 4:11

134 J. R. W. Stott, *God's New Society: The Message of Ephesians*, (Downers Grove: InterVarsity Press, 1979), 168; Liefeld, *Ephesians*, 4:8–12; Gaebelein, Ephesians. 4:12-16; M. Turner, *Ephesians*, *New Bible Commentary*, Vol. 10, (Downers Grove: InterVarsity, 1994), 1238–9.

135 Brown, et. al. *Commentary*, Vol. VI, 469; Green, G. L., *The Letters to the Thessalonians*, (Grand Rapids: Eerdmans Pub, 2002), 261.

136 Kyle Idleman, *Not a Fan: Becoming a Completely Committed Follower of Jesus*, (Grand Rapids: Zondervan, 2011).

137 https://www.stevemurrell.com/7-questions-about-the-value-of-modern-discipleship/.

138 Bonhoeffer, *The Cost of Discipleship*, New York: Touchstone, 1995), 59.

139 *Discipleship vs Talmidim.* Koinonia Institute, http://www.khouse. org/articles/2005/616, 4/21/2019.

140 *Ibid.*

141 More detailed descriptions of Jesus calling the disciples are in Mark 1:16 and John 1:43–51.

142 Gaebelein, Matthew 10:5-6; Leon Morris, *The Gospel According to Matthew*, (Grand Rapids: Eerdmans, 1992),

244-246; R. T. France, *Matthew: An Introduction and Commentary*, (Downers Grove: InterVarsity, 1985), 181–82.

143 Ralph W.Neighbours, *Touching Hearts: Empowering You to Share Your Faith*, (Houston: Touch Outreach Ministries, 2006), 8–11.

144 *What are the Five Types of Fools,* Institute in Basic Life Principles, https://iblp.org/questions/what-are-five-types-fools), 4/8/2019.

145 *Four Spiritual Laws*, https://campusministry.org/docs/tools/Four SpiritualLaws.pdf.

146 *Peace with God*, https://peacewithgod.net/.

147 Robert E. Coleman, *The Master Plan of Evangelism*, (Grand Rapids: Revell, 1993).

148 Jimmy Scroggins, Steve Wright, and Leslee Bennett, *Turning Everyday Conversations into Gospel Conversations*, (Nashville: B&H Books, 2016); https://www.christian- ok.com/turning-everyday-conversations-into-gospel/ jimmy-scroggins/9781462747849/pd/747844.

149 Randy Newman, *Questioning Evangelism: Engaging People's Hearts the Way Jesus Did*, 2 ed., (Grand Rapids: Kregel Publishers, 2017).

150 I found materials by Dr. John MacArthur (http:// www.gty.org/ resources/sermons/80-181/the-parable- of-the-soils) and Dr. Ross Allen (https://bible.org/seriespage/20-parable-sower-and-seed-matthew-13:1–23) to be helpful in unpacking the parable of the soils.

151 *Ten Transferable Concepts*, https://www.cru.org/us/en/train- andgrow/transferable-concepts.html.

152 Roy Comstock and Michelle M. Beck, *Mentoring His Way*, (Christian Mentors Network, 2017), https://www. christianmentorsnetwork.org/.

153 InterVarsity Christian Fellowship,
       https://intervarsity.org/bible- study; Navigators,
       https://www.navigators.org/.

154 "The Wind Beneath My Wings" written in 1982 by Jeff
       Silbar and Larry Henley and first recorded by Kamahl in
       1982.